Crossing North

TRIBULATIONS OF A CUBAN DOCTOR

A Novel

From the author of
Waiting on Zapote Street,
winner of the Latino Books Into Movies Award,
Drama TV Series category

Betty Viamontes

Crossing North
TRIBULATIONS OF A CUBAN DOCTOR

Published in the United States by

Zapote Street Books, LLC, Tampa, Florida

Book cover by SusanasBooks LLC

ISBN: 978-1-955848-16-9
Printed in the United States of America

I dedicate this book to—

Yasek Camacho Alonso, the Cuban physician on whom this story is based, for hours of testimonies and the dozens of pictures that helped me convert this true story into a novel.

The immigrant mothers and fathers who risk it all for their children's futures so that they can live with decency and freedom.

My mother, for showing me that anything is possible.

My beloved husband and my family, for their unconditional support.

My loyal readers, for reading my books and encouraging me to keep writing.

Introduction

I grew up in the shadow of the Cuban Revolution. When I was nine years old, the first wave of exiles arrived in my home state of Florida. These early travelers expected a short stay until the danger passed. They never returned. After the regime banned migration, exiles fled in leaky boats, rafts, and inner tubes. We will never know how many migrants fed the sharks of the Florida Straits. Six decades later, that flow has not stopped. On the contrary, since 1999, over five million Venezuelans have fled communist tyranny, and the Cubans keep on coming.

The geopolitical impact of Castro's revolution is well documented. Few authors, however, have portrayed the desolation that this upheaval brought to individual families. For 21st-century readers, the concept may be hard to understand. Why would a population, nearly as large as New York City, leave their homes, family, and possessions, fleeing into the ocean and jungle? Why would people desert their families forever, knowing that friends had died on the same route? No author has created a more compelling answer to these questions than Betty Viamontes.

In a sense, Betty was born for her task. She was a child of the Cuban Revolution, born five years after Castro seized power. In her teens, she saw her homeland devolve into a police state. Spies infiltrated every block, reporting their neighbors to the political police. Gangs of thugs roamed the neighbor-hoods, threatening and stealing as they pleased. On an island of lush vegetation, basic foods became a luxury. Prisons filled with patriots who dared to question the all-powerful "Comandante." Nobody knew if their family would be next. This was the world in which Betty spent her formative years.

At 15, Betty's family escaped Cuba with only the clothes on their backs. The decades that followed were good to her. Settling in Tampa, she built a family of her own and a successful career in hospital finance. After her mother's death, however, her heart turned to the stories of her youth. She began by adapting her mother's journals into her first novel, "Waiting on Zapote Street." This simple homage to a mother's resilience caught the attention of readers around the world. Its success led to nine other works chronicling the Cuban exile experience. From labor camps to freedom flights, her works became a defining voice for exiled families.

In her latest novel, *Crossing North*, Betty has taken on a more ambitious task. Based on true accounts, she follows the life of a Cuban physician who was exported to Venezuela. His story documents the descent of that oil-rich nation into an impoverished prison-state. Threatened with return to Cuba, his only escape is through desert, ocean, and jungle. The journey is a road of death, peopled with evil coyotes, corrupt officials, bodies, and casual barbarity.

Crossing North is not the record of some distant time—the holocaust or the Inquisition. Its horrors took place in 2021 and 2022, only a few miles from the United States. They have not ended. As I type these words, other families are following this same route. Many of them will fall along the way.

Despite the horrors, *Crossing North* is ultimately a tale of love and family. Its characters are strikingly familiar. They are parents and children like our own, clinging to each other while their world falls apart. Their lives, struggles, and deaths are a lesson and a caution for the modern world.

Nikita Khrushchev once told the world, "History is on our side. We will bury you!" At the time, he headed the USSR, the nexus of global communism. Although Khrushchev is long dead and the Berlin Wall is dust, that threat persists. Despite its spectacular failures, communism continues to entice new generations. Under many aliases, it flows from the lips of politicians from Latin America to Washington, D.C. Six decades after the Cuban Revolution, there is still no greater danger to Western civilization.

Communism is ultimately more a religion than an economic system. Missiles and nuclear weapons offer little protection against its creeds. The only sure protection is knowledge. With this in mind, I commend you to *Crossing North* and the other works of Betty Viamontes.

Allen A. Witt, PhD
Lead Author of *America's Community College: The First Century*

Chapter 1

No Man's Land

The moment the taxi stopped at the checkpoint, I wondered if our journey north would end before it had even begun.

José, our middle-aged cab driver, slowed to a halt when an armed policeman in his twenties stepped into the road and raised his hand.

José, a heavyset bald man, reached for his phone and quickly typed a message. Then he glanced at me in the rearview mirror.

When our eyes met, I noticed a faint smirk.

In that instant, I knew something was wrong.

Moments later, another officer approached. He looked about José's age but carried himself with the authority of someone in charge. Without even glancing at us, he ordered the young policeman who had stopped the car to step aside.

The officer glanced briefly at the phone in his hand, slipped it into his pocket, and walked straight toward my door.

"Get out of the car!" he shouted. "Both of you!"

Leila and I grabbed our backpacks, swung them over our shoulders, and stepped out of the taxi, each of us clutching a large bottle of water.

It was Tuesday, January 25, 2022.

For twelve years, I had lived in the city of Punto Fijo, in the Venezuelan state of Falcón—an important port city with more than 280,000 residents. After deserting my Cuban medical mission without legal work papers, I survived doing whatever jobs I could find, from working as a security guard to assisting as a nurse in a private clinic.

But remaining in Venezuela was no longer an option. Repressive measures had intensified, especially for someone like me, and I feared for my safety. So I sold my used car—one of my few possessions—to begin the journey north with my wife, Leila.

The trip ahead would cover nearly 4,000 kilometers (2,500 miles), but I couldn't think that far ahead. My first challenge was to leave Venezuela.

I had paid the driver $300 for myself and $74 for my wife to take us from Punto Fijo to La Guajira, a remote no-man 's-land near the border between Venezuela and Colombia. We had already traveled more than 270 kilometers.

The La Guajira Peninsula—the northernmost point of South America—is a hot, arid region with few highways. The Caribbean Sea borders it to the north and the Gulf of Venezuela to the southeast. The Guajira Desert, as it is known in Colombia, had become one of the main gateways for Venezuelan migrants entering Colombia—a chaotic place where smugglers operated openly.

I had been charged more than my wife because I was a Cuban doctor trying to escape. The alternative could have been a Venezuelan jail—or worse, deportation back to Cuba. José had assured me the higher price would guarantee my safe passage across the border.

I should have known better than to trust someone recommended by a friend of a friend.

Chapter 1

Later, I would learn that the driver had chosen the most dangerous crossing because he never intended to keep his promise.

After our five-hour journey from Punto Fijo, the officer slapped the taxi's windshield and motioned in a circular gesture for the driver to turn around. José nodded, shifted the 2001 Ford Fiesta into reverse, and once he was about fifty meters from the checkpoint, made a U-turn and drove away.

When the cab disappeared into the distance, panic began to rise inside me, though I did everything I could to keep Leila from noticing.

The officer ordered us off the road toward a shaded area. Two younger officers followed behind him.

My heart began to pound as we walked across reddish clay soil dotted with patches of dry grass. I inhaled slowly, trying to remain calm, while Leila and I exchanged anxious glances.

"Stand behind that big tree!" he barked. "And no sudden movements. You hear?"

We nodded and obeyed.

I could hear the crunch of our footsteps and the occasional chirping of a bird. Red dust lifted into the air as we walked.

"Stop right there and turn around!" he ordered.

That was when I realized we were far enough from the road that no one could see us.

We stood facing them, frightened, beads of sweat forming on our foreheads. The two younger officers looked at my Venezuelan wife in a way that made my stomach tighten.

Chapter 1

"Where are you going?" the man in charge asked.

"To Colombia," I answered.

"Sir, I have a sick uncle in Colombia and need to see him," Leila added quickly. "We mean no harm."

She tucked a strand of her highlighted hair behind her ear. At thirty-eight, she was still as beautiful as when we met—brown eyes full of kindness and the curvy figure Cuban men admired.

We had been together for nearly ten years, but we had married only a few days earlier. Until recently, we had been unable to find anyone willing to marry us. Before our departure, however, Leila found a notary who—after some persuasion and a fee—agreed to perform the ceremony despite my having only a Cuban passport.

"If you want to cross into Colombia," the officer said coldly, "you need to pay."

"How much?" I asked, trying to remain calm. Although I had mastered the Venezuelan accent after years there, I feared my nervousness might reveal the Cuban accent I had worked so hard to hide.

Later, I would realize that our driver's message had already exposed me.

"Twenty-five hundred dollars."

I stared at him in disbelief. It was an outrageous amount—a small fortune in this part of the world.

"But we don't have that kind of money," I protested.

"Either you pay," he replied, "or we tie you up and beat you until you find a way to get it."

"Please, sir," I said quietly. "Just let us go."

4

Chapter 1

At that moment, I feared not for myself but for my wife—and for my inability to protect her.

"How much do you have?" he demanded.

My mind raced through all the places we had hidden our money: inside a Bible, sewn into the hem of a blanket, tucked into my wife's bra, hidden in our clothes. I also carried about $200 in my wallet.

"I don't know," I said. "Not that much."

I pulled the cash from my wallet and handed him the $200.

"We need more," he said. "Put down your bags."

A knot tightened in my stomach.

I had known this journey would be dangerous when we decided to leave.

But I never imagined the danger would come so soon. Anything could have gone wrong on this trip.

And now it had.

Chapter 2

The Beginning

I was born in Placetas, a municipality in Villa Clara Province in central Cuba, in 1983—twenty-four years after the triumph of Castro's revolution and four years after my sister Gloria was born.

Villa Clara itself was created in 1976, when the old province of Las Villas was divided into three: Cienfuegos, Sancti Spíritus, and Villa Clara. Santa Clara, once the capital of Las Villas, became the capital of the new province.

Villa Clara lies in the heart of the island, blessed with beautiful beaches along its northern coast and fertile land that once supported numerous sugar mills. Yet the elegance of its colonial architecture struggled to survive decades of neglect. Over time, deterioration often won.

Placetas, with fewer than 75,000 residents, sits along the Carretera Central, the highway that runs the length of Cuba from east to west. Its main Catholic church honors the town's patron saint, San Atanasio de Placetas.

I grew up in a modest one-story house with a crumbling stucco façade and interior walls covered in peeling paint. The living-dining room held only a few pieces of simple furniture: several rocking chairs and a square wooden table with four chairs.

Chapter 2

Despite the hardships of life in Cuba, I had loving parents and a grandmother who spoiled me as much as she could in a country where the food we could buy with our ration card seemed to shrink every year.

My childhood was not easy. My mother cooked over a fire of firewood behind the house. When toys arrived in the stores—usually once a year—she waited in lines that sometimes lasted more than a day to buy one for me. Often we could not afford them, so many of my toys were made by my father and me from pieces of wood.

I loved playing baseball or spinning a *trompo*, watching the wooden top whirl across the ground.

My favorite meal was *congrí*—rice cooked with black beans and spices—served with pork, malanga chips, and fried yucca. But I only ate it when we visited relatives in San Gregorio. One of them owned a small farm that had somehow escaped confiscation during the agrarian reforms of the 1960s.

At home, most days we ate boiled green plantains with tomato purée. Sometimes there was nothing else.

Growing up, I didn't always have shoes for school. One year, they were too big. Another year, I had to wear my sister's old pair. I remember walking into class embarrassed, convinced everyone would notice.

No one did.

My father never learned how to swim, yet he insisted on teaching me. He took me to the Zaza River and stood on the riverbank shouting instructions.

"Come on, Joel! You can do it!"

Chapter 2

That was how I learned to swim at five years old.

Sometimes he took me on his bicycle to watch the trains pass. I loved standing beside him near the tracks while we counted the cars as they thundered by.

Afterward, he would place his arm over my shoulder.

"You're destined for great things," he would say. "Never forget that."

I didn't understand what he meant, but his words stayed with me.

My father worked as a primary school teacher and part-time university instructor. My mother was a laboratory technician. Even as professionals, their salaries were not enough to feed our family.

Many nights we went to bed hungry.

To earn extra money, my father sometimes worked a few hours in the fields. My mother bought soap or shampoo in the city and sold them secretly on the black market. Sometimes she even organized illegal raffles.

Anything to put food on the table.

In those days, even a bar of soap was a luxury.

When I was eleven, in 1994, I began working in the fields during my summer vacations. A full day of labor earned me twenty pesos—about twenty cents.

By then, Cuba had entered the *Special Period*, the economic crisis that followed the collapse of the Soviet Union and the end of its subsidies. Food shortages worsened, and many of my father's friends left the island on makeshift rafts. Some were lost at sea.

Chapter 2

The government, desperate to increase food production, began distributing small parcels of land to farmers.

The owner of the farm where I worked refused to pay me at first because I was too young. So I offered to work for a snack—sugar water and a piece of bread.

One day, I cut my finger badly while working. When I saw the blood, I panicked. The farmer suggested we go to a doctor, but I wrapped the wound with a rag and kept working.

I wanted to prove I was strong.

Eventually, impressed by my determination—and encouraged by the other workers—the farmer began paying me.

Although my father avoided political discussions at home, I slowly began to understand the reality of our country through conversations among relatives.

My father was too afraid to criticize the government openly.

He also remained silent when school officials forced me to wear the red scarf that marked me as a "Pioneer for Communism," or when teachers made us chant revolutionary slogans praising the system.

But I was not a communist.

Neither was my father.

As soon as I left school each day, I removed the red scarf and stuffed it into my pocket—my small act of rebellion.

My uncles often talked about the United States. They said people there were free and could criticize their government without being jailed.

I began imagining what life there might be like.

Chapter 2

Soon, I began to have recurring dreams. In the dream, I finally reached the United States and felt overwhelming joy. But suddenly a door closed in front of me, leaving me trapped outside.

My resentment toward the Cuban government grew stronger after I learned about my father's cousin, Julio—a family secret that had long been hidden from me.

Julio had been a soldier under Fulgencio Batista, the dictator who fled Cuba on December 31, 1958. In the early years of the revolution, many soldiers who failed to escape were executed by firing squad.

Julio managed to avoid capture for several years while working quietly as an electrician. But in 1973, someone recognized him and reported him to the authorities.

For two years, he endured psychological torture. Guards repeatedly blindfolded him and threatened to execute him. They fired their weapons into the air, watching him collapse in terror.

For two years, he lived believing that one day the gunshots would be real.

In 1975, while my parents were on their honeymoon, they learned that the last time the guards had blindfolded Julio and threatened him, his worst fear had finally come true.

Chapter 3

The Decision

When I started high school, the government sent my classmates and me to work in the fields for forty-five days as part of *La Escuela al Campo* (Schools in the Fields). We worked for free on land that the government had expropriated from my grandfather.

My grandfather had arrived in Cuba from the Canary Islands long before Castro came to power. Over the years, he gradually acquired small parcels of land, earning his living from farming. After the revolution, those lands were confiscated.

Now I was forced to work them.

My job consisted of harvesting potatoes and pulling weeds from around tomato plants in the fields of San Gregorio. Teachers watched us carefully to make sure we didn't eat the tomatoes. Many times I thought about grabbing one to replenish my energy, but I didn't dare take the risk. My dream of attending the university would have been destroyed if a teacher had caught me. Only students with an exemplary record were allowed to continue their education.

While working those fields, I often thought about my grandfather, whom I knew only through photographs. I also remembered my father's words when he took me to watch the trains pass and told me I was destined for great things.

Chapter 3

What better way to make a difference, I thought, than by becoming a doctor and saving lives?

But medicine was also a means to an end.

I didn't want to stay in Cuba. I didn't want to drown at sea, like some of my father's friends who had attempted to escape on rafts. The only realistic way to leave the island was through Cuba's international medical missions.

So I studied hard. I stayed focused and disciplined, and learning came naturally to me. I understood that my ability to absorb knowledge could one day mean the difference between life and death for someone. I never took that responsibility lightly.

By the time I graduated with a degree in Emergency Medicine, Cuban doctors had become the country's most valuable export. The government earned more than ten billion dollars a year sending them abroad, mainly to Africa and the Caribbean.

Doctors had become another commodity—no different from sugar or cattle.

Inside Cuba, however, doctors lived like everyone else: poor. Occasionally, a grateful patient might offer a small gift—a jar of guava marmalade or a can of condensed milk—but such gestures were rare luxuries.

Working abroad could significantly increase my income, but money was not my main motivation.

When I was twenty-seven, shortly after graduating from the University of Villa Clara, I left Cuba on a medical mission to Venezuela. My plan was simple: once abroad, I would find a way not to return.

Before leaving, I spoke with my parents.

Chapter 3

They were both in their fifties and had spent most of their lives under the communist system. They knew their chance to leave Cuba had long passed.

"Son," my father said, "I always told you that you were destined for great things. And now you're a doctor. But I know your future is not here."

He sat in a rocking chair in our living room. My mother sat nearby, quietly wiping away tears.

"We didn't raise you for ourselves," he continued. "Go and do what you were meant to do. If you stay here and speak your mind, you could end up beaten—or in jail. That's why so many young people have left."

He paused.

"You have no wife or children. Your only ties here are your parents, your sister, and your grandmother. Your sister has her family. Your mother and I are getting old. You must think about your future."

"Viejo, my goal is to get you out," I said. I often called him *Viejo*—old man—a term of affection.

"We are not going anywhere," he replied firmly. "We need to stay with your sister and our grandchildren. You do what you must. And when you reach your destination, remember those of us who remain in this godforsaken place. Pray for us."

My father had aged prematurely. Deep grooves marked his cheeks. His thin body and sunburned skin reflected the long hours he spent working in the fields to supplement his income. Resigned to a life with no real future, he looked exhausted.

Cuba was still suffering from the aftermath of the *Special Period*, the economic collapse that followed the Soviet Union's collapse. Overnight, the island had lost nearly 80 percent of its imports, including food, fuel, and medicine.

Food disappeared from the shelves. Trucks occasionally arrived in neighborhoods carrying yucca or other vegetables, and the long lines often turned violent. Transportation broke down, agriculture collapsed, and the country was forced into so-called "organic farming," which drastically reduced productivity.

For many Cubans—including my friends—the Special Period never truly ended.

By the time I was preparing to leave in 2010, the scars of that era remained everywhere.

I felt as though I were drowning in Cuba.

And I needed air.

At that time, there were no migration routes through Nicaragua or Guyana. Those paths would open years later. For me, the only way out was through the medical mission in Venezuela.

Leaving my parents behind broke my heart.

But I didn't want to wake up thirty years later and find myself trapped in the same hopeless life they had endured—waiting, praying, and hoping for a change that might never come.

Chapter 4

The Medical Mission

MAPA POLÍTICO
Estados, capitales y principales ciudades

- DISTRITO FEDERAL
- EDO. ANZOÁTEGUI
- EDO. AMAZONAS
- EDO. APURE
- EDO. ARAGUA
- EDO. BARINAS
- EDO. BOLÍVAR
- EDO. CARABOBO
- EDO. COJEDES
- EDO. DELTA AMACURO
- EDO. FALCÓN
- EDO. GUÁRICO
- EDO. LARA
- EDO. MÉRIDA
- EDO. MIRANDA
- EDO. MONAGAS
- EDO. NUEVA ESPARTA
- EDO. PORTUGUESA
- EDO. SUCRE
- EDO. TÁCHIRA
- EDO. TRUJILLO
- EDO. YARACUY
- EDO. VARGAS
- EDO. ZULIA

I climbed the stairs to the airplane at José Martí International Airport in Havana with a mixture of excitement and fear. I had never flown before.

After settling into my window seat, I looked around the cabin. Many of the doctors traveling with me seemed just as wide-eyed as I was. Some smiled nervously as they examined their surroundings. One read a book, perhaps trying to calm his nerves.

Chapter 4

Another, seated across the aisle by the window, stared silently at the runway. I wondered what he was thinking—and who he was leaving behind.

When the airplane finally lifted off, my thoughts drifted back to my childhood. For a moment, I imagined myself running across the white, cotton-like clouds outside my window. Then I looked down toward the sea, searching for land.

I could no longer see Cuba.

A wave of guilt washed over me. I was saving myself—or so I believed—but the people I loved most, my greatest treasures, remained behind in Villa Clara. As I had done many times before, I tried to analyze my situation. Slowly, logic overcame emotion.

If I wanted to help them one day, I first had to save myself.

During the flight, I barely spoke to the doctor sitting beside me. Small talk seemed pointless. What were the chances I would ever see any of these people again?

After about two hours, we landed at Maiquetía "Simón Bolívar" International Airport in Caracas, Venezuela, where we stayed overnight. The next day, we were assigned to different parts of the country. I was sent to Punto Fijo, on Venezuela's northwestern coast.

Punto Fijo had been founded in the 1940s after two large oil refineries—one operated by Standard Oil and the other by Shell—brought jobs and economic growth to the region. The city enjoyed a warm climate year-round, with temperatures ranging from about 23°C (73°F) in the winter to 31°C (87°F) in the summer.

Chapter 4

Soon after arriving, I met the person in charge of my brigade and learned that I would be working at a CDI—Centro de Diagnóstico Integral (Center for Integral Diagnosis). These clinics were part of a joint program between the Cuban and Venezuelan governments that provided free medical care in underserved communities. They included a 24-hour emergency room, laboratory services, radiology, endoscopy, and other basic medical services staffed by Cuban and Venezuelan doctors.

It didn't take long for me to learn that Cuban doctors received only a fraction of what their Venezuelan counterparts earned. Venezuelan physicians were paid more in two weeks than we received in an entire month. Even worse, roughly 80 percent of our salary was deposited into a Cuban bank account that we could not access until we completed the mission and returned to Cuba.

During my first three months in Punto Fijo, I had nowhere to live. I slept in a shared room reserved for on-call doctors. Rest was nearly impossible because physicians kept entering and leaving the room throughout the night.

Shortly after I began working at the CDI, I faced one of the most difficult moments of my young career.

One night, while I was the only doctor on duty, seven wounded patients were brought in almost simultaneously—some with gunshot wounds, others with knife injuries. Their relatives surrounded me, shouting and begging me to help.

For a moment, I didn't know where to begin.

Chapter 4

Then I took a deep breath and began triaging the patients, asking a clerk to escort the relatives outside.

A nurse who had herself been hospitalized at the clinic stepped in to help, along with another nurse on duty that night. As we worked frantically to stabilize the wounded, a man burst into the room screaming.

He rushed toward the patient I was treating.

"Don't save that son of a bitch!" he shouted, gesturing wildly with his hands.

I ignored him and continued working.

"Doctor, didn't you hear me?" he yelled again.

He appeared to be in his mid-twenties. His blue shirt hung open, torn and stained with blood. When he stepped closer, I finally noticed the gun in his hand.

I instinctively stepped back.

"I need security in here now!" I shouted. Then I turned to him. "Please leave and let me treat this patient."

"If you save him," he said coldly, "I'll kill you."

I raised my gloved, bloodstained hands and waited.

Finally, two security guards rushed in, weapons drawn.

"Put down your gun!" one of them shouted.

I stepped farther away, bracing myself for the possibility of a shootout.

"This is none of your business!" the man yelled.

"You need to let the doctor do his job," the guard replied. "Leave now."

Several tense moments passed before the guards managed to persuade him to leave.

Once he was gone, I returned to the wounded patients.

That night, only weeks after arriving in Venezuela, I began to question whether I should remain on the medical mission or return to Cuba. This was not what I had expected.

The living conditions added to my anxiety.

At the beginning of my fourth month in Venezuela, four of us moved into a small abandoned house not far from the clinic. It had only one bedroom and unfinished cement floors. The bathroom tiles were so filthy that I had to scrape away the hardened grime with a knife. But at least we didn't have to pay rent.

With the help of our neighbors, we began fixing the place. We painted the walls, repaired the roof, and cleaned the rooms. Some neighbors even donated used furniture—a refrigerator, a television, and a stove.

Just as the house finally became livable, the brigade supervisors inspected it and ordered us to move out. They reassigned the house to someone else.

We were relocated to a communal residence with four bedrooms shared by sixteen people—far too many for such a small space. Each room had four beds, but sometimes even more people were squeezed in.

Roma, a thin woman with a stern expression, supervised our brigade and lived with us. She made the rules clear from the beginning: we were not allowed to make any derogatory comments about the Cuban government—not even during our free time.

The regulations were detailed in Resolution No. 168 of 2010 issued by Cuba's Ministry of Foreign Trade and Foreign Investment. The document imposed strict limits on our freedom of movement, association, and speech.

We were forbidden from forming meaningful relationships with Venezuelans. Doing so was considered a violation of the rules. If our supervisor reported us for criticizing the Cuban government, questioning the program, or interacting too closely with locals, our mission could be terminated.

If that happened, we would lose everything.

The Cuban government would keep the money we had earned.

Our schedule consisted of 24 hours at the clinic, followed by 24 hours of "rest." But the rest days were not truly rest. During that time, we were required to conduct home visits and see as many as 150 patients to meet the program's quotas.

Often, I carried no medical equipment—not even a stethoscope. My real task was to collect names so the Cuban government could document the visits and receive payment.

For each doctor, Venezuela paid Cuba approximately $5,000 per month—often in the form of oil.

Even on our supposed rest days, we had a curfew. We were forbidden to be outside after six in the evening.

The Cuban government justified these restrictions by reminding us that our education had been free.

Chapter 4

That was when I realized something important.

In Cuba, nothing that is free is truly free.

The price is paid in other ways.

Our supervisors also required us to attend Communist Party meetings and participate in acts of repudiation against any doctor who defected from the mission. We were expected to condemn them publicly.

This was not what I had imagined when I left Cuba.

I had believed that becoming a doctor would open the door to freedom. Instead, I had discovered that even thousands of miles from home, the system I had tried to escape still controlled my life.

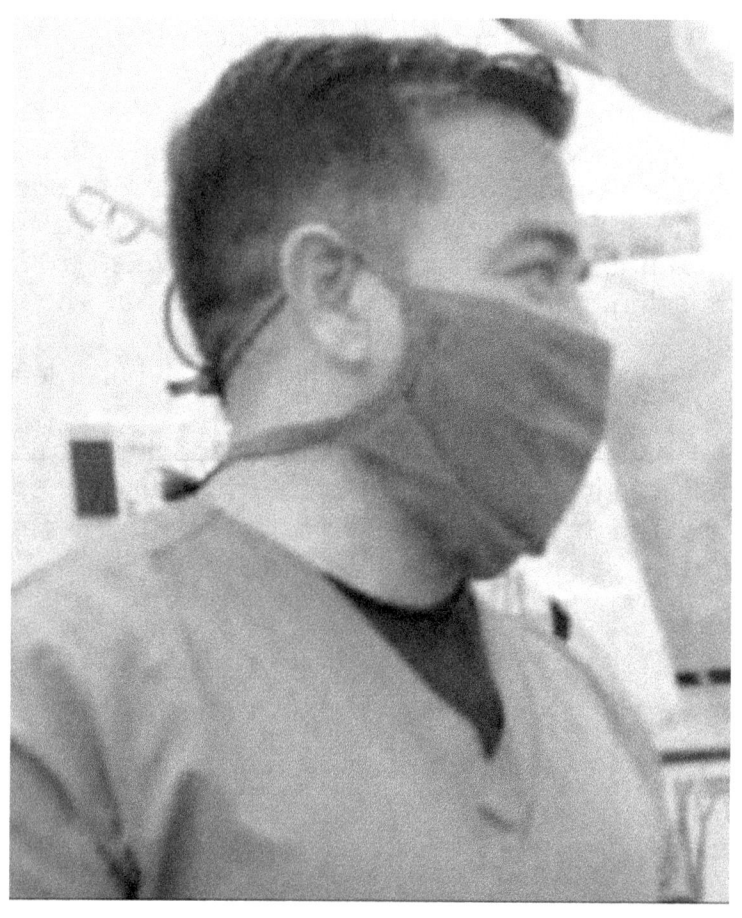

Chapter 5

Leila

While working at the clinic, I met Luisa, a middle-aged woman with diabetes and hypertension. She also cared for her epileptic son, who had been confined to a wheelchair since childhood after suffering a stroke. Among the many patients I saw each day, Luisa was the kind of person one never forgets.

"My love, can I bring you some soup?" she would ask when I visited. "Look at the bags under your eyes. Are you sleeping well?"

The usual distance between doctor and patient meant nothing to her. She spoke to me the way a mother speaks to her son, always worrying about whether I was eating enough or working too hard.

Her oldest daughter, Celia, usually drove her to her appointments. Before long, Celia and I became friends.

My immediate concerns were controlling Luisa's diabetes and treating a plantar lesion that had developed because her condition was poorly managed. I was also trying to find a treatment that might reduce the frequency of her son's seizures.

Because of these problems, I began visiting Luisa's home regularly to change her bandages and check on her son. Each visit felt less like a house call and more like returning to a family home.

"Joel, look," she said during one visit, greeting me at the door with a warm smile. "I made soup for you. Next time you come, I'll cook the beans you like so much."

She spoke softly, with the calm patience of someone who had endured many hardships and learned to carry them quietly.

"Luisa, this is my job," I told her. "You don't need to cook for me."

"Nonsense. Sit down and eat, my love."

She always called me *my love*. As I ate, she would sit across from me at the small kitchen table, watching with satisfaction while she told stories about her children.

I admired what she had built. She had raised five children—three sons and two daughters—and despite the country's economic struggles, they remained a close and loving family.

Luisa rarely spoke about politics or the country's worsening situation. But in private, Celia sometimes confided in me how much the rising cost of living was hurting her mother. Inflation had reached 27 percent in 2009 and climbed even higher the following year.

Still, Luisa accepted life as it came.

Since Hugo Chávez was elected president in 1998, Venezuela had undergone a profound transformation. In 2004, Chávez and the National Assembly took control of the Supreme Court, weakening one of the country's last institutional checks on executive power. Slowly, constitutional protections began to erode.

By 2010, the country was already sliding into a serious economic crisis brought on by falling oil prices and years of mismanagement. Yet at the time, few of us realized how much worse things would become.

Despite these hardships—and despite my repeated protests—Luisa continued feeding me whenever I visited. Sometimes she even brought food to the clinic on days when she didn't have an appointment.

One night, shortly after midnight, my phone vibrated with an urgent message from Celia.

Please hurry. It's my brother. His convulsions won't stop. Please come now.

Afraid she might call and wake the other doctors sleeping in the room, I replied quickly: *Received.*

But as soon as I sent the message, I hesitated.

Leaving the house at night to treat a patient violated the strict rules imposed on Cuban physicians assigned abroad. If I were caught, I could be reported and sent back to Cuba.

For a moment, I stood there, staring at the screen.

Then the answer became obvious.

I was a doctor.

It was two in the morning. Three other doctors were asleep in the room. I slipped quietly out of bed, crossed the cold floor barefoot, and eased open the front door.

Celia's house was only a few streets away. If I moved quickly, I might be able to help her brother and return before anyone noticed I was gone.

Before leaving, I grabbed a few medical supplies.

When I arrived, Celia and Luisa were in a state of panic, trying desperately to restrain the convulsing twenty-three-year-old in his wheelchair.

"Step aside," I said calmly.

"I'm sorry," Celia said, her voice trembling. "I know about your restrictions. I was asleep when Mami called me. I came as fast as I could. If anyone can help him, it's you. Will you get in trouble?"

"Don't worry," I said. "This is more important."

I focused on the young man, working carefully until the violent seizures finally subsided and his breathing began to slow.

When it was over, the room fell silent.

Celia and Luisa hugged me, thanking me again and again. Before I left, Luisa tried once more to feed me.

"No, thank you, Luisa," I said gently. "You both need to rest."

Outside, the street was quiet.

Most of the small houses had red tile roofs and low ceilings. In daylight, the neighborhood seemed modest but peaceful. At night, it was something else entirely.

I was walking through what locals called a *zona roja*—a red zone where robberies and shootings were common.

Few people dared to be outside at that hour.

As I walked, thinking about the patient and hoping no one at the doctors' residence had noticed my absence, a man suddenly stepped out of a dark alley between two houses and struck me.

"Give me your wallet!" he shouted.

Adrenaline surged through my body.

Before I could think, my fist was already moving. I struck him in the face with all my strength. He collapsed onto the pavement.

Chapter 5

For a split second, I thought the danger was over.

Then I saw the gun.

And the second man standing behind him.

"Look, I'm sorry," I said quickly, raising my hands. "I'm a Cuban doctor. I just came from treating a patient. Let's forget this happened."

"You think you're tough?" the second man said.

"No," I replied. "I'm not tough. Listen—I don't make much money."

"I don't care. Give me your money."

The man I had punched slowly climbed to his feet while his partner kept the gun pointed at my chest.

With one hand raised, I reached slowly into my pocket.

"Don't try to be brave again," the first man warned.

I nodded.

"Here," I said, handing him my wallet.

He grabbed it. Moments later, the two men disappeared back into the alley.

Shaken but relieved to still be alive, I continued walking.

When I finally returned to the house and saw that everyone was still asleep, I quietly closed the door behind me and let out a long breath.

***

About a month later, Luisa injured one of her fingers and needed surgery. Her surgeon asked if I could assist during the procedure.

Chapter 5

Before the operation, I stopped by Celia's house to check on her.

When I arrived, Celia greeted me with a hug.

"Joel, let me introduce you to my sister Leila."

Leila was Luisa's youngest daughter. She lived about twelve kilometers away, near one of the oil refineries, but she had come to stay with her mother before the surgery.

Unlike me, she carried herself with easy confidence. She approached with a bright smile.

"Thank you for taking care of my mother," she said.

Then she studied me curiously.

"Do you work out?"

I nodded.

Before I could react, she reached out and squeezed my biceps.

"Wow, doctor," she said with a playful grin. "Look at those muscles."

At the time, I didn't realize she was flirting. I understood that only much later. Back then, I was too focused on the strict rules governing our mission.

If I wanted to begin a relationship with a woman, I would first need permission from my brigade supervisors. Without it, they could transfer me to another city—or even send me back to Cuba.

The regulations treated relationships as if they could be scheduled and approved in advance.

But real relationships didn't work that way.

To truly know someone required time—time to discover whether a connection could survive the pressures of life. The system made that nearly impossible.

Chapter 5

Because of those restrictions, I had no intention of starting a relationship.

And yet, the moment Leila walked into the
room, something in my life quietly began to change.

Chapter 6

Joel
(Leila)

The moment I saw Joel, something in me paused. I noticed everything at once—his blue eyes, his dark hair combed carefully back, and the shy way he stood there as if he didn't quite know what to do with himself. There was something endearing about that shyness. It made me smile.

I could immediately tell he wasn't Venezuelan. The way he dressed, the way he held himself—it was different.

So, I decided to break the ice. Otherwise, the silence would have been unbearable.

After introducing us, my sister was standing next to him in the living room. Joel gave me a polite nod, clearly unsure how to respond.

"Do you work out?" I asked.

Before he could answer, I reached out and touched his biceps.

He turned so red that I burst out laughing.

We exchanged a few polite words, but he remained guarded, almost as if he didn't realize I was flirting with him.

I found that even more charming.

***

Chapter 6

I didn't see Joel again until about a month later, on the day of my mother's surgery.

I was sitting in the waiting room, scrolling through my BlackBerry to pass the time, when he finally walked out of the operating room.

My heart jumped a little when I saw him.

He came over and sat beside me.

"She's doing well," he said calmly. "She's recovering now. It will be a little while before you can see her, but don't worry."

Relief washed over me.

While he spoke, I noticed him fiddling with his phone.

"Let me see that," I said, reaching for it.

The phone looked ancient. Several of the keys were broken.

"My God," I said, laughing softly. "This thing belongs in a museum."

"I'm sorry," he said quietly.

That made me feel terrible.

"No, no," I said quickly. "Don't apologize. I've just never seen a phone like this before."

Then I asked, "Are you on Facebook?"

He looked at me with complete confusion.

"Facebook?" he asked. "What's that?"

I stared at him, then burst out laughing. "You're serious?"

He nodded.

I shook my head in disbelief.

"Give me your phone," I said. "I'm fixing this situation immediately."

He watched me with curiosity as I created his account.

When I finished, I handed the phone back.

"There," I said proudly. "Now you officially exist in the modern world."

He looked at the screen.

"What is it for?" he asked.

"It's social media," I explained. "You can talk to people and share pictures."

"Why?"

I laughed again.

"Because it's fun."

"If you say so."

***

Trying to keep the conversation going, I asked, "So what are you doing for Mother's Day? It's coming up."

"My mother lives in Cuba," he said quietly. "I wanted to call her that day, but we don't get paid until the end of the month. So it will have to wait."

For a moment, I thought I had misunderstood.

"You mean you can't call your mother because you can't afford a phone card?"

He nodded.

"I thought doctors made good money," I said.

"Not Cuban doctors."

The way he said it was so simple, so matter-of-fact.

But it broke my heart.

They were exploiting him, and he didn't even seem to realize it.

In Venezuela, we could buy phone cards that allowed international calls. Using the number on the card, an operator would connect the call to Cuba.

So, I bought one.

Chapter 6

On Mother's Day, Joel called his mother.

He was embarrassed when I gave him the card, but he accepted it. When he finally spoke to her, the gratitude in his voice was unforgettable.

Later, his mother thanked me, too.

After that, she and I began speaking often, as if we had known each other for years.

***

After my mother recovered, I returned to my apartment, but Joel and I stayed in touch by phone.

I was busy with work, but I made time to see him whenever I could—usually once a month.

One day, some friends and I planned to go to the movies, and I invited him.

"I can't go," he said. "I have restrictions, and also..."

I knew exactly what he meant.

"Don't worry about the money," I said. "Come with me. You work too hard. We'll go early so you won't get in trouble."

After some hesitation, he agreed.

Still, I didn't want him to feel embarrassed in front of my friends. In Venezuela, it was customary for men to pay for the women.

While we stood in line, I quietly slipped some money into his pocket and leaned close.

"Check your pocket," I whispered. "I put money there so you can buy the tickets."

He looked down, shaking his head, clearly uncomfortable.

"Don't worry," I said softly. "No one will know."

Chapter 6

After that day, something between us changed.

We talked more easily. He relaxed when he was with me.

At first, we kept our relationship secret.

Whenever Joel came to check on my mother, we would exchange glances across the room but couldn't even hug. My brothers were strict and didn't want me dating anyone—especially someone in Joel's situation.

But the more I got to know him, the less that mattered.

Nothing was going to stop me from seeing him.

Sometimes he told me stories about his childhood.

"When I was little, there were many times I didn't have shoes," he said once.

He described how his father had traced his feet onto a piece of wood and cut the shapes to make homemade sandals.

"When we played hide-and-seek," he said, smiling slightly, "I was always the first one found because my shoes made so much noise."

Listening to him was almost surreal.

As a child in Venezuela, I had toys, clothes, and everything I needed.

He had almost nothing.

I couldn't understand how someone could grow up like that.

Over time, I found myself defending him—to my family, to friends who looked down on him for being Cuban, and eventually even to some of his coworkers.

Many Venezuelans blamed Cubans for what was happening in our country. They believed Cuba had exported its political system into Venezuela, and Joel represented everything they resented.

But Joel was nothing like the image people had in their heads.

He had opposed communism since childhood.

And he was one of the kindest men I had ever met.

When I finally told him I was divorced and had two children—Marcos and Julián, four and six years old—I was terrified he would walk away.

But he didn't. Not even for a second.

Despite everything—our responsibilities, his restrictions, and the constant transfers ordered by his supervisors—we stayed connected.

He never complained about the moves or about the tiny salary he received.

Growing up in poverty had taught him to expect very little from life.

But I wanted something different for him.

I wanted to fight for him.

I wanted to show him that life could be bigger than the one he believed he deserved.

Chapter 7

Luisa
Joel

A doctor friend of mine told me about a bed that had become available where he lived in Creolandia, on the second floor of a physician's office. I would have to walk an hour to work each way, but living with only one other doctor would give me more freedom. We could cover for each other when one of us needed to step away from the suffocating restrictions imposed on us.

I could no longer endure the same routine day after day, especially being locked inside after six in the evening during our so-called "rest time." When I spoke privately with doctors I trusted, many of them agreed with my assessment of our situation, and what we were experiencing felt like a modern form of slavery.

And the more people I lived with, the stricter the rules became. Too many eyes watching.

It took some time to convince my supervisors that I should move, but eventually they granted my request.

Creolandia was one of the sectors of Punto Fijo. Its name came from the nearby Amuay refinery, which had been called *La Creole* in the 1940s. Like many neighborhoods in Punto Fijo, Creolandia struggled to preserve its sense of community despite rising crime and violence.

Chapter 7

"An hour is too far from work," Leila warned me. "Anything can happen during that walk."

But as time passed, even the gang members in the area began to treat me with respect. I had helped many of their relatives during illnesses, and word traveled quickly.

Not long after I moved to Creolandia, Leila invited me to a birthday party at a friend's house. Her mother, Luisa, her sister Celia, and their families would also be there.

I spoke with my roommate, and he agreed to cover for me during the evening check.

For the first time in a long while, I could go out without constantly worrying that someone would discover I had broken the rules.

When we arrived at the party, the house was filled with laughter and music. Some people danced; others sat talking and drinking beer; others moved between the kitchen and the backyard with plates of food.

I wasn't much of a dancer, but Leila grabbed my arm and pulled me toward the dance floor.

I felt awkward dancing in front of so many strangers, but she laughed and encouraged me. Seeing her smile made it impossible to refuse.

When she danced, her whole face lit up. Her joy was effortless and genuine. Being with her and her family gave my life something I had been missing for a long time—a sense of normalcy.

After dancing for a while, we sat down with some of her friends, drank a couple of beers, and talked about the situation in Venezuela.

Those who didn't know me simply called out, "Oye, Cubano!"

Chapter 7

For once, I allowed myself to relax. I could breathe again.

But as the night wore on, everything changed.

I was talking with a group of Leila's friends in the backyard when Celia suddenly rushed outside. Her hands moved nervously as she spoke, her voice fast and panicked.

"Joel, please come inside. It's Mami. Something is wrong. She hasn't been feeling well all day but insisted on coming to the party. She was sitting on the sofa, took a sip of beer, and suddenly collapsed. She won't wake up. Please hurry!"

I ran inside with Celia and Leila close behind.

When I entered the room, Luisa was slumped on the sofa, unconscious and drenched in sweat.

"Please do something!" Celia cried. "Don't let her die!"

People stepped aside as I pushed through the crowd.

Luisa wasn't breathing.

I checked her pulse. Nothing.

"We need to get her on the floor!" I shouted.

A man helped me lower her onto the tiles.

I began chest compressions.

One. Two. Three.

"Oh my God," Leila cried. "Joel, please—don't let Mami die!"

"I'm a nurse," a young woman said, kneeling beside me. "I'll help."

She began mouth-to-mouth resuscitation while I continued compressions.

Luisa's body felt heavy and lifeless beneath my hands.

"Come on," I whispered under my breath.

Chapter 7

I performed thirty compressions and paused.
I checked her pulse, but nothing.
I started again. I did thirty more and paused.
Still nothing.
"Joel!" Celia cried.
I kept going.
My arms burned, and sweat ran down my face.
Then I checked again.
A faint pulse.
"There it is," I said. "She has a pulse!"
Relief swept through the room. But it didn't last long.
Her pulse faded again.
"We need to get her to the hospital—now!"
We were far from the clinic where I worked—and even if we had been close, I couldn't take her there. If I did, my supervisors would discover I had violated the mission's rules.
So we rushed her to the nearest facility, a private hospital.
Julio, one of the party guests, and I carefully placed Luisa in the back seat of his Silverado truck. I climbed in beside her.
Within moments, she lost her pulse again.
I immediately resumed chest compressions.
"Hurry!" I shouted at the driver. "We don't have much time!"
The first hour after a heart attack—the golden hour—often determines whether a patient survives.
Ten minutes later, we arrived at a private facility called *Clínica Especializada*.
Two healthcare workers rushed out with a stretcher and brought Luisa inside. I followed as a

nurse asked her daughters to remain in the waiting room.

"I'm a doctor," I said.

The nurse nodded and allowed me to accompany them into the emergency room.

Within minutes, I realized the attending physician was moving too slowly.

I resumed cardiac massage.

"I need a heart monitor now!" I said sharply.

The doctor handed it to me. I quickly placed the leads on Luisa.

Her heart was beating, but the rhythm was irregular—consistent with an acute myocardial infarction.

"We need to move her to the ICU," the doctor said.

"She's not stable," I replied. "If we move her now, she could die on the way."

But he insisted.

As the stretcher rolled down the long hallway toward the intensive care unit, I continued resuscitation.

When we arrived at the ICU, I turned to the nurse.

"I'm a doctor. Please give me a sterile coat so I can assist."

"We don't have any available," she replied.

"What about those?" I asked, pointing to a rack.

"Sir, you need to stay outside."

"At the very least," I said, trying to remain calm, "I need to know her blood pressure, pulse, and oxygen saturation."

A few minutes later, the nurse returned.

Chapter 7

"Her oxygen saturation is fifty," she said.
"Was she intubated?" I asked.
"I don't think so."
"Then tell the doctor he needs to intubate her immediately. Her oxygen saturation is below fifty. That's standard protocol."
She went back inside. Moments later, she returned.
"She's been intubated."
Although physicians from other facilities were often allowed to assist, I had a strong suspicion as to why they refused to let me in.
They had heard my accent.
In Venezuela, Cubans were blamed for everything that had gone wrong in the country.
They didn't know that I had left Cuba because I opposed the very system they believed I represented.

***

Despite everything we did, Luisa never regained consciousness.
A few hours later, another heart attack took her life.
When the doctor came out of the ICU and delivered the news, Celia and Leila collapsed into tears.
"I'm sorry," he said. "We did everything we could."
I looked at him in silence. My expression said what I could not.
I didn't believe him.
I embraced Celia and Leila as they cried.
Inside, I felt hollow.

Chapter 7

As hard as I had fought to save her, it wasn't enough.

And that night, in trying to help the woman who had treated me like a son, I had broken several of the mission's rules.

Soon, I would have to face the consequences.

Chapter 8

The Visit

I was in my office reading a patient chart when Orlando, the physician in charge of the CDI, walked in and sat down across from me.

We both wore white coats, but the middle-aged man looked far more rested than I felt. A musky cologne lingered around him.

"Good afternoon," he said.

"Good afternoon," I replied, setting the chart aside.

He studied me for a moment.

"Is there something you need to tell me?"

"About what?"

He leaned forward, resting his elbows on his knees. Then he clasped his hands together and interlaced his fingers.

"It has come to my attention that you are engaging in prohibited relationships with nationals," he said. "A woman comes here bringing you food. And recently, you took a patient to a private clinic."

His eyes narrowed.

"Why didn't you allow the family to take the patient themselves?"

"If I had done that," I said, "the patient would have died on the way. She was unstable."

"But she died anyway."

The words hung in the air.

I wondered how he knew so much. Perhaps a nurse had overheard my conversation with one of the doctors.

"That was beyond my control," I replied.

He placed his interlaced fingers beneath his chin.

"So you're simply ignoring the rules."

He leaned back in his chair.

"Listen carefully. If this continues, I will transfer you out of the state. You could also be sent back to Cuba. If I were you, I would reconsider my actions."

"Understood," I said.

There was nothing to gain by arguing. He was in charge. He controlled where I lived, where I worked, and even whether I could remain in the country.

An uncomfortable silence followed as he stared at me with open distrust.

"What else should I know?" he asked.

"What do you mean?"

"I hear you are dating a national."

"We are getting to know each other," I said. "That's why I haven't requested permission. It's too soon."

"Do you understand that this is not allowed?" he said sharply. "You must request permission and receive authorization from your superiors beforehand."

I inhaled slowly and clenched my fist inside the pocket of my white coat.

"I understand that what I did may not have been appropriate," I said carefully. "It wasn't my intention to break the rules. The timing of the request for permission wasn't right. I needed time to know whether the relationship had a future."

"And you think you determine the timing?" he snapped.

His voice hardened.

"The rules already determine the timing. What makes you think you can redefine them?"

He leaned closer.

"You are here because we allowed you to be here. Because the Revolution did you a favor. You should be grateful to the Revolution."

Anger rose in my chest. I felt my face growing warm.

In that moment, I was reminded of a truth we all understood but rarely said aloud: my medical degree, my work, even my presence in Venezuela did not belong to me. They belonged to the system that had sent me there.

I needed this conversation to end.

Silently, I began counting backward in my head, forcing myself to remain calm.

"I'm sorry for my actions," I finally said, my voice flat. "And I am grateful to the Revolution for this opportunity."

"Fair enough," he said, standing up.

He adjusted his coat and looked down at me.

"I don't want to have to come back here again. The next time I do, things will be different."

He paused.

"Do I make myself clear?"

"You do."

He turned and left the office.

The door closed behind him.

For a moment, I sat in silence.

Chapter 8

Then I grabbed the patient chart I had been reading and slammed it onto my desk.

Chapter 9

The Funeral

Luisa's funeral followed a traditional three-day service, during which relatives from different parts of the country came to pay their respects. In Venezuela, families typically choose between holding the viewing at a funeral home or at their own house. Luisa's family chose the latter—a less expensive option that also allowed greater flexibility for relatives and visitors. The viewing lasted two days, with the burial taking place on the third.

Leila wondered how I would manage to attend, given the restrictions placed on Cuban doctors. I spoke with several colleagues, and they agreed to cover my shifts. Even so, I knew I was taking a risk. If Orlando found out, he could make my life even more difficult.

In preparation for the visitors, the family prepared a large pot of soup and several trays of *Toddy*—a fortified chocolate powder mixed with hot milk.

"Take some warm Toddy," I heard Celia and Leila say as they moved around the room offering cups to relatives.

Many visitors also drank rum while sharing stories about Luisa's life. I found that unusual. Drinking hard liquor during a funeral was not something I had seen in Cuba.

Throughout the house, people remembered Luisa for her kindness and generosity. One by one, her children spoke about their mother—everyone except Raúl, her wheelchair-bound son.

"Mamá always made us believe that anything was possible if we worked hard," Leila said.

"It's true," Celia added. "She made us feel invincible."

"And she made the best Toddy," Leila's youngest son said.

Laughter briefly filled the room.

Many people shared stories of how Luisa had helped them—watching their children, bringing food when someone in the family was sick, or simply offering comfort during difficult times.

While the adults talked, the children played in the backyard and around the house. At one point, Marcos, Leila's youngest boy, tugged on his mother's sleeve.

"Mami, I'm bored."

"Respect your grandmother," Leila whispered.

The boy walked away, stomping his feet in quiet protest. He was more restless than his older brother, who preferred to sit quietly with a notebook, drawing, and coloring.

Raúl, Luisa's twenty-three-year-old son, remained visibly anxious throughout the service. Sitting in his wheelchair, he watched everything with sad, attentive eyes. The stroke he had suffered as a child had left him unable to speak, but he could answer yes or no by moving his head. Despite his limitations, he understood everything happening around him.

The casket had been placed in Luisa's bedroom, and people moved in and out of the room throughout the day.

Chapter 9

At first, Raúl refused to leave his mother's side.

After a few hours, Leila pulled a chair beside him and spoke softly to him. From where I sat, I couldn't hear what she was saying, but I saw her place an arm around his shoulders, gently caressing his back.

Eventually, he nodded.

She wheeled him into the dining room and served him some soup and Toddy. He swallowed with difficulty, but at least he did not require a feeding tube.

Before the viewing began, Leila had introduced me to her family as her boyfriend. She no longer wanted to hide our relationship.

Her two older brothers argued with her at first. But after she explained how I had risked my position to help their mother, their attitude softened. Celia also spoke on my behalf.

During the gathering, several relatives asked me about my family and life in Cuba.

"How does Venezuela compare to Cuba in terms of natural beauty?" one relative asked.

I smiled.

"Do you know what Christopher Columbus said when he landed in Cuba in 1492?" I asked. "He said, *'This is the most beautiful land that human eyes have ever seen.'*"

"That's because he hadn't discovered Venezuela yet," one of Celia's friends replied with a grin. "That happened on his third voyage."

"In 1498," I said.

"You know your history," someone else remarked.

Chapter 9

Leila's older brothers listened carefully to everything I said, observing me with quiet scrutiny—as if trying to determine whether I was worthy of their sister.

On the third day, during the burial, her brothers and I helped carry Luisa's casket to the gravesite.

When the ceremony ended, Leila's oldest brother approached me and extended his hand.

"Thank you for caring for my mother," he said. "And for risking yourself to try to save her life. We're also grateful for everything you've done for my brother. You managed his seizures better than the other doctors."

"It was the least I could do," I replied.

Luisa had always said she was a spiritual woman.

Leila had told her about our relationship and about her brothers' doubts.

As I watched the family gathered around the grave—speaking quietly, supporting one another—I couldn't help wondering if Luisa was somehow still there with us, holding her family together one last time before beginning her life in the house of the Lord.

Chapter 10

Defection - 2012

After Luisa's funeral, my superiors ordered me to move back into the house where sixteen doctors and nurses lived. The brief freedom I had enjoyed in Creolandia vanished overnight. Living again under constant supervision left me frustrated.

Around that time, Leila began spending more time at her mother's house, caring for her disabled brother. Her siblings helped when they could, but after Luisa's death, Raúl began to decline. His seizures became more frequent, and his visits to the clinic increased.

None of the treatments I prescribed worked anymore, and eventually I referred him to a neurologist. Being away from my own mother had been painful enough. I could only imagine what Luisa's absence meant for someone like Raúl, who had depended on her for everything his entire life.

We all missed her.

Leila often woke in the middle of the night, calling for her mother, wishing she could see her again.

Not long after those dreams began, she started bringing me lunch and dinner during my shifts.

"You don't have to do that," I told her. "You already have enough on your plate."

"Mami would have wanted me to," she said. "She always worried about you."

"It's only natural," I joked. "I'm very lovable."

She laughed and nudged me.

I knew her bringing food to the clinic could create problems with Orlando. But I was tired of living in fear. I decided I would no longer let his threats control me.

Orlando returned several times to warn me about my relationship with Leila. But as my second year in Venezuela came to an end, I began to push back—not only by ignoring his warnings but also by questioning the mission itself.

One day, I said to my supervisor, "What we're doing isn't right. We could be helping people instead of just collecting names on a page."

Roma, who oversaw our group, looked at me carefully.

"So, you don't believe in the mission of the Revolution?" she asked.

"That's not what I said. I've shown you the numbers. On my rest day, I'm expected to collect demographic data from 100 people. There's barely time to treat anyone."

She said nothing.

"When I became a doctor," I continued, "I wanted to save lives, not fill out forms. We're expected to process 150 patients in a single day. That's impossible. Doctors end up fabricating information."

Roma shook her head and laughed quietly.

"I hear you loud and clear," she said. "You break the rules, and now you think you can tell us how to run the operation."

"That's not my intention. I'm trying to help my patients."

Chapter 10

"You clearly have ideas inconsistent with those of a good revolutionary," she said coldly. "Maybe this is not the right place for you."

The next day, Orlando appeared in my office. He remained standing.

"This will be brief," he said. "In two hours, you will return to the house, collect your belongings, and prepare to leave. Your time in the mission has ended."

I stared at him.

"But why? I'm just trying to do my job."

"You've been given many opportunities to follow the rules," he said. "You continue to break them."

Then he walked out. I sat there, stunned as I realized he was sending me back to Cuba.

The moment had come. I couldn't wait two hours.

Fifteen minutes later, I left the clinic.

When I reached the house, no one was there. I packed only a few essentials and slipped out before anyone could return.

Luisa's house would be the first place they would look for me. I needed to disappear.

My first refuge was a friend's home while his parents were away. I stayed four days. When they returned, I had to move again.

That night, I walked toward a small park and sat alone on a bench.

The park was empty.

For the first time since leaving the mission, fear settled in.

Would I ever see my parents again?

Chapter 10

I thought about calling them, but I had no calling card—and even if I did, what would I say? It would only fill them with worry.

It was better to wait.

After sitting there for a while, I called Celia.

She answered immediately.

"What are you waiting for?" she said after hearing my story. "Come here right now. We'll find a place for you."

"Are you sure?"

"Of course."

"Maybe talk to your husband first."

"He'll be fine with it," she said firmly. "Just come."

I walked to her house that night.

For two weeks, I stayed with Celia and her family. After that, I moved several times—sometimes with other doctors who had defected, sometimes with friends I had made during my time in Venezuela.

Once I was sure no one was searching for me anymore, I began looking for work.

I took whatever jobs I could find—driving, cleaning, anything that paid.

But I missed medicine.

Some friends warned me not to look for work in healthcare. They said it was too risky.

I ignored them.

One day, I walked into a small private clinic.

"I'd like to speak with the owner," I told the receptionist.

"He's busy."

"I'll wait."

Nearly two hours passed before she returned.

Chapter 10

"The doctor will see you now."

The white-haired physician looked at me across his desk.

"What brings you here?"

"I'm looking for work. Any work. Cleaning, office work—anything."

"But the receptionist says you're a doctor."

"I am," I said. "A Cuban doctor who defected from the mission."

He studied me for a moment.

"I cannot hire you as a physician. To practice here, you would need to revalidate your degree."

My heart sank.

"But I could hire you as a nurse."

My eyes lit up.

"Really?"

"Under the table."

"That would be incredible."

"Be here tomorrow at nine."

"I will," I said, shaking his hand.

The next morning, I arrived early.

After a brief orientation, I began working as a nurse.

I gave the job everything I had.

Even though I could no longer practice as a doctor, caring for patients again gave my life meaning.

Over time, the clinic owner grew impressed with my work. One day, he told me he had watched me through the security cameras and liked how I treated the patients.

Eventually, he made me a promise.

Chapter 10

He would help pay for the process to revalidate my medical degree—and even support me in pursuing a specialty.

But none of that could happen without proper identification.

And obtaining it would require me to take a step I had never imagined.

Chapter 11

Reincorporation - 2015

From the time I defected until 2015, life became somewhat more normal. Leila, her children, and I visited other cities in Venezuela, went to the beach, and enjoyed simple outings like going to the movies without worrying about curfews or restrictions. For the first time in my life, I felt a sense of freedom.

Yet freedom, I learned, is a relative term.

I was living in the shadows—working under the table at the mercy of those willing to risk giving me a job, driving without a license, and paying bribes whenever the police stopped me. What troubled me most was knowing that the small comforts we enjoyed came largely from Leila's salary, not mine. I could not practice medicine legally or earn a doctor's wages.

Working unofficially meant poor pay that struggled to keep up with Venezuela's growing inflation.

In 2013, after the death of Hugo Chávez, Nicolás Maduro came to power. Many Venezuelans refused to recognize him as the legitimate president. Opposition grew as he passed laws that consolidated his power, weakened his rivals, and moved the country toward a one-party system.

That same year, inflation rose to 40.64 percent, nearly twenty points higher than the year before.

Chapter 11

In 2014, inflation climbed above 60 percent—the highest in Venezuela's history and among the highest in the world. Maduro attempted to control the crisis by cutting spending and raising the minimum wage, but the measures failed. In 2015, inflation soared to 181 percent, shattering both national and global records.

That year, Cuban doctors who had deserted the medical mission but were still living in Venezuela were contacted by colleagues who remained in the program. Through the professional organizations we all belonged to, they relayed a message from the Cuban government.

We were told to return to the mission—or face prosecution and forced repatriation to Cuba.

Many of us returned.

Fear played a role, but so did something else: a promise. We were told that if we rejoined the mission, we would receive Venezuelan identification cards. With proper documentation, I could revalidate my medical degree and legally practice medicine in Venezuela—this time without being controlled by the Cuban government.

The possibility of working again as a doctor was difficult to ignore.

My goal was never to remain in Venezuela forever. Eventually, I hoped to leave the country, but to do that, I needed money.

When I rejoined the mission, however, my salary dropped dramatically. I now earn the equivalent of about $40 a month, paid in Cuban convertible pesos (CUC), which I later exchange for Venezuelan currency. Before defecting, I had been earning about $200.

Chapter 11

Most of that difference resulted from the rapid devaluation of Venezuela's currency. On top of that, I no longer received the additional payments that doctors who had never defected continued to receive from the Cuban government.

Even within the mission, we were treated differently.

During staff meetings, reincorporated physicians were rarely allowed to speak.

"No, no," our supervisor would say. "Those who were reincorporated will speak at the end of the meeting."

But the meetings always ended before our turn came.

Shortly after returning, my superiors confiscated my red passport.

That passport was essential for applying to a special parole program that allowed Cuban doctors to seek entry into the United States.

Whenever I asked about my Venezuelan identification card, my supervisor reassured me.

"It won't be long," he would say. "Your number is coming up."

I waited.

Months passed.

Then more months.

Eventually, I realized the identification card was never coming.

In desperation, I tried applying for a U.S. visa using my blue passport. A few months later, I received a letter from the U.S. Embassy informing me that my application could not be approved without the proper documentation—the red passport that had been taken from me.

Only then did I understand.

The Cuban government had planned this all along.

By promising me identification and taking my passport, they had removed my only realistic chance to escape.

I wrote letters to U.S. Congresswoman Ileana Ros-Lehtinen and Congressman Mario Díaz-Balart in Miami, pleading for help. They replied that there was little they could do while I remained in Venezuela.

After rejoining the mission, I was no longer subject to the six o'clock curfew. But I was forbidden from leaving the state.

Cuban authorities worked closely with Venezuelan officials to monitor doctors like me and prevent us from crossing state lines. Of course, in Venezuela, almost anything was possible for the right price. Bribes flowed freely through the police and government.

But traveling across state lines required money—and I needed to save every dollar I could.

By then, I knew that the next time I crossed state lines would have to be the last.

To save money, I worked as much as possible. After finishing my shifts at the clinic, I drove my small car late into the night, taxiing passengers around the city.

Months turned into years.

My identification card never arrived.

At one point, the Cuban government stopped paying the reincorporated doctors for six months. One colleague confronted our supervisor.

"We haven't been paid," he said.

Chapter 11

"You haven't been paid because you are from Villa Clara," the supervisor replied. "There have been delays for doctors from that province."

"But several doctors here are from Villa Clara," the man protested. "Some were paid. Others weren't."

"You need to be patient," the supervisor said calmly. "Remember—the Revolution never abandons its children."

When I heard statements like that, I clenched my fists.

I wanted to speak.

I wanted to say what everyone was thinking.

But I stayed silent.

Speaking out had already cost me dearly once before, and I had no intention of drawing attention to myself again.

I felt trapped.

As long as I remained in Venezuela with only my blue passport, I could not obtain a work permit or a driver's license. I would always be forced to work under the table, living at the mercy of others.

I existed in a strange limbo—not fully Venezuelan, no longer truly Cuban, and without the documents that could allow me to build a life anywhere else.

On paper, I was almost invisible. A doctor without a license. A citizen without a country.

A ghost moving quietly through the edges of society.

Chapter 12

The Pandemic

After my reincorporation, I moved in with Leila, Raúl, and the boys. At the time, they were eight and ten years old. Despite my demanding schedule—working for the mission during the day and driving a taxi at night—I helped Leila with the children whenever I could.

We tried to make Raúl feel included in our daily routine. When Leila and I sat on the sofa in the evenings, talking with the boys about their day, we would wheel him into the living room so he could join the conversation.

But no matter how hard we tried, Raúl never adjusted to life without his mother.

By 2017, he seemed to lose the will to keep fighting. His health declined rapidly, and he died one month before his thirtieth birthday.

The loss devastated Celia and Leila, who had carried most of the burden of caring for their brother. The thought that he had reunited with their mother in Heaven brought them some comfort, but it took both sisters a long time to recover. For months, they could not speak about Raúl without breaking down.

Life moved quickly during those years, consumed by family responsibilities and work. I slept little and worked long hours, but I had no choice.

Chapter 12

Venezuela was entering one of the worst economic crises in modern history.

By 2017, hyperinflation had shaken the country after years of growing deficits and falling oil revenues. In 2018, inflation was estimated at 80,000 percent. The government repeatedly removed zeros from the currency to make it appear stronger, even though nothing supported its value.

Nearly ten percent of the population fled the country.

When we went to the stores, we often found empty shelves. The few available goods rarely had price tags. Prices changed so rapidly that they were calculated only at the register.

As the bolivar lost value, imports became increasingly expensive, pushing the country deeper into economic collapse.

Maduro's response was to print more money and impose strict exchange controls. These policies drove people to convert their bolívares into U.S. dollars, creating a thriving black market for foreign currency.

The situation became so absurd that some of Leila's friends joked it was cheaper to use bolívares as toilet paper than to buy actual toilet paper.

Crime in our neighborhood decreased somewhat as many criminals left the country in search of better opportunities elsewhere.

Meanwhile, Leila and I saved every dollar we could.

By 2019, four years after my reincorporation, we began seriously planning our departure from Venezuela. Leaving would require careful planning and a significant amount of money. We discussed every possible scenario.

But life rarely unfolds the way we imagine.

In March 2020, Venezuela confirmed its first official cases of COVID-19.

Even before the pandemic, the World Food Program estimated that 32 percent of Venezuelans suffered from food insecurity. The situation worsened dramatically once the virus arrived.

On March 12, Maduro declared a public health emergency, suspending public gatherings and flights from Europe and Colombia. Some people were even arrested for allegedly spreading "false news" about the virus.

By the end of that month, China had sent one million rapid test kits to Venezuela.

Maduro later agreed to include Venezuelan citizens in trials for the Sputnik V vaccine, and by December 2020, the government had secured doses for roughly ten million people.

Despite these announcements, doctors on the ground were not prepared to handle the crisis. Hospitals lacked the most basic supplies.

At times, it felt like we were working in a war zone.

The government attempted to project a different image to the outside world. Television crews filmed deliveries of medical supplies to the CDIs—boxes containing a few pairs of gloves, surgical masks, or bottles of paracetamol. After filming, the same supplies were sometimes taken to another clinic for another staged delivery.

This atmosphere of control may explain why Doctors Without Borders suspended its operations in Caracas in November 2020, following government restrictions.

Some medications were available in private pharmacies, but they were far beyond the reach of ordinary Venezuelans. The average monthly salary had fallen to between three and four dollars, while a single day's dose of enoxaparin—a medication used to prevent blood clots—cost twenty-five dollars.

That first year of the pandemic was devastating.

Many of my patients died without the possibility of receiving proper care. Doctors were under a gag order, but some still spoke out about the reality we faced: overcrowded clinics, no ventilators, and shortages of even basic items like paper to record patient histories.

Healthcare workers themselves became victims of the virus. According to *Médicos Unidos*, more than two hundred Venezuelan healthcare workers died from COVID-19, although the government reported different numbers.

Maduro's strategy was to control the narrative and silence criticism through intimidation.

While the situation in Venezuela was terrible, conditions in Cuba were even worse.

I feared constantly for my parents' health. They still lived in Villa Clara, where healthcare conditions were far poorer than in Havana. When people developed COVID symptoms, they often waited in line for hours outside clinics only to be sent home without treatment.

Many relied on home remedies—lemon juice, honey, saltwater gargles, and sunlight. Pneumonia often became a death sentence because antibiotics were scarce.

Several of my parents' friends died.

Fortunately, the money I had sent them before the pandemic helped them survive the worst months. Even so, both of them eventually became infected.

Those were some of the longest nights of my life.

I called them every day. I also contacted neighbors and promised to send them gifts if they brought my parents food—especially chicken soup. Anything that might help them recover.

Thankfully, my parents had a small reserve of aspirin, vitamins, and antibiotics that I had sent earlier for emergencies. Those supplies, along with the kindness of their neighbors, helped them pull through.

By 2021, natural immunity and vaccinations had begun to reduce COVID-19 cases in Venezuela, and many restrictions were lifted.

For the first time in months, the country felt as if it could breathe again.

For Leila and me, that moment meant something else.

It meant the window we had been waiting for was finally opening.

The time had come to leave Venezuela.

Chapter 13

July 11, 2021

On July 11, 2021, despite the risk of imprisonment and beatings, thousands of people in Cuba took to the streets demanding freedom. Protests erupted across the island as citizens denounced the repression and economic misery under the government of Miguel Díaz-Canel.

Within hours, videos filmed on cell phones spread across the world. For the first time in decades, Cubans were openly chanting for liberty.

The images sparked solidarity abroad. In cities across Italy, Spain, the United States, and other countries, people gathered in support of the demonstrators.

As soon as I heard about the protests, I called my parents.

My father answered.

"Papi, please don't go out," I said immediately. "I don't trust them. The government won't take this lightly. Please stay home with Mami."

He sighed.

"Son, I'm tired of waiting for change," he said. "Everyone here is exhausted. Look at the people in the government—fat and healthy. The rest of us are just surviving."

I could hear voices in the background, people shouting in the streets.

"They say either the pandemic will kill you," he continued, "or the government will—through hunger or a beating. So people have decided they would rather die standing than live like this."

My chest tightened.

"Viejo, please," I said quietly. "I can't lose you, not like that. Stay home. Do it for me."

For a moment, he didn't answer.

"I don't know, son," he said finally. "This might be our only chance."

"Please put Mami on the phone," I said. "I love you."

When my mother answered, her voice sounded calmer.

"Mami, don't let him go out," I told her. "I know how these people think. They won't tolerate this. Please keep him home."

"Don't worry," she said softly. "Your father talks big, but I know how to handle him."

I smiled despite the tension.

My father always believed he was the one in charge of the house.

But my mother had spent a lifetime quietly proving otherwise.

The unprecedented protests quickly became the main topic of conversation among Cuban doctors abroad. In the professional groups where many of us communicated, people grew unusually bold. Some even began posting their opinions publicly on Facebook.

One colleague wrote on a professional forum that it was time to stand on the right side of history.

"I know some of you may disagree," he wrote. "And I respect your opinion. I hope you respect mine. I support the protesters in Cuba."

He should have known the consequences.

Chapter 13

Around two in the morning, Venezuelan and Cuban officials arrived at the house in Punto Fijo where he lived with other doctors. They had come to take him to jail.

But my friend had anticipated this.

By the time the officials arrived, he was already in Colombia.

Meanwhile, in Cuba, the government began identifying protesters through videos posted online. Many were arrested—some of them children. Reports soon emerged of disappearances, beatings, and harsh interrogations.

Some detainees were released months later, but many carried deep physical and emotional scars. Some were so traumatized that they were afraid to leave their homes.

Thankfully, my father had listened to my mother.

They stayed inside that day, praying for the protesters' safety.

But the consequences of July 11 did not stop at Cuba's shores.

In Venezuela, repression also intensified. Rumors spread that reincorporated Cuban doctors—especially those who had previously defected—would soon be arrested or sent back to the island.

For someone like me, being sent back to Cuba was worse than prison.

It felt like a death sentence.

And I knew one thing with absolute certainty.

I could not let them take me back.

Chapter 14

The Children

While finalizing our plans to leave Venezuela, the question of the children surfaced again—as it did every time we discussed the journey north.

"We can't take them with us," Leila said quietly. "I'm afraid for their safety. But I can't leave them here either. I have to get them out of Venezuela."

I couldn't argue with her. The trip north could cost us our lives—a risk I was willing to take. But the boys had their entire lives ahead of them.

After they obtained their passports, Leila began calling relatives and friends to explore possible destinations. After weighing several options, she decided to send them to Argentina.

Although Argentina had a strong socialist party, it had not experienced the level of government control that had consumed Cuba and Venezuela. Its president had been democratically elected, and private property remained largely protected. Still, I worried that the same political cancer that had spread through our countries could eventually reach there as well.

For now, it was the safest option.

The journey would take six days by bus. The route began in Caracas and crossed several

countries—Colombia, Ecuador, Peru, and Bolivia—
before reaching Argentina. The passengers would
have to change buses multiple times along the way.

The night before their departure, anxiety kept
me awake. I worried about their safety and wondered
how long it would be before I saw the boys again.

Over the six years Leila and I had lived together, I had watched them grow from small children
into young men. I helped them with their homework,
took them on family outings, and listened when they
had problems at school. They had a father, but they
often came to me for advice.

I liked to believe I had become something like
a second father to them.

That evening, before going to the bedroom I
shared with Leila, I walked toward the boys' room.
Their suitcases were already packed and sitting on
the floor. Marcos and Julián sat on the edge of their
beds talking quietly.

I stood in the doorway.

"All packed?" I asked.

They nodded.

"I'm going to miss you both," I said. "You know
that, right?"

They nodded again, but neither of them said
anything.

"I hear Buenos Aires is a beautiful city," I continued, trying to keep my voice steady. "Maybe one
day, if things change for me, I'll come visit you there.
Or maybe you'll come visit me somewhere else."

I looked down. I had always been terrible at
goodbyes.

Before I could say anything else, Marcos stood
up and walked over to me. He wrapped his arms

around me in a tight hug. After he stepped back, Julián did the same.

"Well," I said, wiping a tear before they could notice, "you should get some sleep. You have a long trip tomorrow. Take care of yourselves—and take care of your mom. You'll be the men of the family on this trip."

"You're not going to be here when we leave?" Marcos asked.

"I have to go to work in a few hours," I said. "I'll already be gone. I'm going to try to get some sleep now."

"Good night."

"Good night."

As I turned to leave, Marcos asked one more question.

"What are you going to do with Victoria?"

Victoria had come into our lives in 2015. She was a white, fluffy dog with pink ears who had been abandoned on our doorstep when she was only a few months old. From the beginning, she followed me everywhere around the house.

We suspected she had been abused. Whenever the doorbell rang, she would run to my room and hide under the bed.

The boys loved her. We took her to the park, played ball with her, and slowly she became part of our family.

"When we leave, your aunt will take care of Victoria," I said. "She'll be in good hands."

Marcos shrugged without answering. I knew both boys would miss her—and me.

That was the last conversation I had with them.

Chapter 14

The next morning, I left the house before dawn.

I told myself that Leila and the boys would be safe. They were traveling on a large bus with reclining seats, air conditioning, and even Wi-Fi. I assumed the journey would be uncomfortable, but manageable.

What I failed to consider was that the bus company did not control the police.

Leila didn't tell me what happened during the trip until almost three weeks later. She didn't want me to worry.

A few hours after leaving Caracas, the bus stopped at one of the many military checkpoints along the road. Most of the passengers were asleep.

Suddenly, a scream woke Leila.

"What are you doing?" a woman shouted. "Take your weapon away from my son! He's only thirteen!"

Leila opened her eyes and froze.

A skinny guard—no older than twenty—stood in the aisle holding an AK-103 rifle, its barrel pressed against the chest of the boy sitting in front of her.

Terrified, Leila wrapped her arm around Marcos.

"Please," the bus driver pleaded. "Leave the boy alone. He isn't doing anything."

The guard didn't move.

He stared angrily at the mother and her son.

Leila felt her heart racing. She was ready to throw herself over Marcos if the rifle turned toward him—but she knew she could not protect both boys at once.

The man holding the rifle looked barely older than a teenager. He carried a weapon far heavier than the responsibility he understood.

"Please, sir," the mother whispered, her voice trembling. "He's just a child."

For a moment, no one spoke, and the entire bus held its breath.

Finally, the young guard lowered his rifle and stepped off the bus. Leila realized she was shaking.

A few seconds later, another officer outside signaled the driver to continue, and the bus pulled away.

Weeks later, when Leila finally told me what had happened, I tried to imagine myself sitting there beside her.

If that rifle had been pointed at one of the boys in front of me, I'm not sure I would have been able to control myself.

Chapter 15

Victoria

I had already been separated from my parents and my sister for eleven years. Yet I still couldn't build the emotional walls necessary to protect myself from getting hurt again.

For that reason, I never wanted to grow too attached to Victoria. I knew how painful it would be to leave her one day.

I have always loved animals. They depend entirely on us for their care, and I take that responsibility seriously.

Despite the country's harsh conditions, we fed Victoria well and cared for her as if she were one of the family. One afternoon, however, while we were at the park, a stray dog approached her and began to play.

Leila's children were still young and didn't think much about how dirty the stray looked. They happily let Victoria run around with him while Leila and I sat on a nearby bench talking.

When I finally noticed the other dog, I called the children over. But by then it was too late.

Victoria had been infected with ticks.

Over the next few days, her health deteriorated quickly. She became lethargic and developed a fever. Soon she stopped eating and began vomiting. Diarrhea followed.

Victoria had contracted ehrlichiosis, a bacterial infection transmitted by ticks.

Chapter 15

As the disease progressed, her spleen became inflamed, and fluid began to accumulate in her abdomen.

If I didn't intervene, she was going to die.

She would look at me with those sad eyes, as if silently asking for help.

So I did what I could. At home, I performed an emergency paracentesis to remove the excess fluid from her abdomen and began treating her with doxycycline.

During those difficult days, as I nursed her back to health, something changed between us.

Victoria became deeply attached to me—and I to her.

Somehow, she always seemed to know when I had returned from a stressful day at work. She would greet me at the door, wagging her tail, and in a moment manage to lift the weight from my shoulders.

Our bond only grew stronger over time. She became my emotional support and I her devoted protector.

Which is why I knew that leaving her behind would be one of the hardest things I would ever do.

As our departure date approached, Victoria seemed to grow quieter.

Sometimes she would sit beside me and watch me in silence.

It was almost as if she understood what was coming.

Chapter 16

Married

It took us a long time to find someone willing to marry us, but eventually we did—a notary who had a small office about three kilometers from our home. We found her only three days after Leila returned from Argentina.

But Leila wasn't feeling well.

The stress of the long trip had weakened her immune system, and she soon tested positive for COVID-19. Within days, she developed all the typical symptoms: cough, headaches, fever, fatigue, and loss of taste.

I treated her as best I could. After three weeks, she began to recover and slowly returned to her normal routine.

Our departure from Venezuela was approaching quickly, and we wanted to be married before we left. That became our next priority.

There was no reception, no party. We had been living together since 2015, and it was December 27, 2021. Every dollar mattered now—we needed to save as much as possible for the journey ahead.

We dressed the way we might for a trip to the movies.

Leila wore blue jeans and a navy blouse with three-quarter sleeves. Her long brown hair, streaked with highlights, fell loosely over her shoulders. I wore black pants and a long-sleeved shirt with a gray pattern she had given me for my birthday.

Leila looked radiant.

She kept making jokes, and I laughed like a teenager. She had a way of bringing color to my otherwise gray life.

When we stood facing each other, I looked into her brown eyes. There was an intensity in her gaze—a quiet fierceness, like that of a lioness protecting her pride.

In that moment, words were unnecessary.

I saw her determination, her courage, and her promise to stand beside me no matter what came next.

Celia and her husband, Carlos, served as our witnesses. They had always been there when we needed them most.

The room where we were married looked more like a classroom than a ceremonial hall. Long tables and simple chairs filled the space. The notary—a middle-aged woman with glasses and black hair pulled into a ponytail—asked the official questions.

We answered and recited our vows. Then we signed our names in a large registry book resting on one of the tables.

After the notary said that we were officially married, Leila and I kissed.

Beside us, her sister quietly wiped away a tear.

When we stepped outside, the sun was shining, and the sky seemed impossibly blue, dotted with thick white clouds. Electrical wires stretched between two tall poles, cutting across the view.

A white house with a clay-colored roof stood nearby. Beyond it, a garden burst with red and violet flowers.

Chapter 16

I walked over, plucked a lilac flower from the garden, and handed it to Leila.

The notary smiled and snapped a photograph.

In the picture, Leila stands holding the flower, her sister and brother-in-law beside us, all of us smiling in the afternoon light.

It was a simple moment.

But it would become the last truly happy moment we shared in Venezuela.

Chapter 17

The Call

I sat on the sofa beside the end table, waiting for my parents to reach the neighbor's telephone.

I could almost picture them as they walked there—both now nearing their sixties, thin and worn down by years of long lines, blackouts, and an empty refrigerator. Yet I could still imagine hope in their eyes and their unwavering faith in God.

"God will provide," my mother always said.

"Joel?" Her voice sounded like an angel when she came to the phone—soft, caring, comforting.

"Vieja," I said.

I called her *old lady*, a term that carried far more affection than the words themselves suggested. It honored her motherhood, her sacrifice, her quiet strength.

"How are you and Papi doing?"

She inhaled deeply.

"What can I tell you, my love? We're always waiting for your call. We live to hear you say you're well... that you're happy."

"I'm fine," I said. "In fact, Leila and I got married. I haven't spoken to you in a couple of months and didn't have time to write."

"You got married?" she exclaimed, her voice bursting with joy. "Oh, my God! You have no idea how happy that makes me. At last! I thought it would never happen."

"Everything happens in God's time, Vieja. You know that."

"Yes, I've always said that," she replied. Then she turned away from the phone and called out, "Lorenzo! Our son got married! Can you believe it?"

In the background, I heard my father's voice.

"Really? Married, married?"

I smiled.

"Yes, married!" my mother confirmed.

"Tell him congratulations," my father said.

"I heard him, Vieja," I replied.

"So," she continued, her voice light again, "any honeymoon plans?"

"About that..." I paused and took a slow breath, choosing my words carefully. "Vieja, I have a project coming up. You may not hear from me for a while. I don't know how long. But I'll call you as soon as I can."

"Is everything okay?" she asked.

"It is," I said quickly. "Do you need me to send you anything?"

"No," she replied. "You already do more than enough for us. And now that you're married, you need to worry about your wife."

"If you ever need anything, you know I'll find a way."

She sighed.

"A cousin of yours sent us some powdered milk, chicken, beans, and a few other things—even coffee. Your grandmother used to say that before the revolution, we had the best coffee in the world. Now we barely have any at all."

She paused.

"We stretch the little we can get. That's what we do."

"One day, Vieja," I said quietly, "when I reach my goals, you won't have to stretch anything. I'll send you all the coffee you want. I swear you'll never be hungry again."

"Ay, mijo," she said softly. "My good son. You've always been a dreamer. Sometimes your ideas sound crazy... but when you believe in something, you make us believe too."

Her voice softened.

"I hope God hears you, my son. I hope He's listening."

Tears rolled down my face.

Even when I closed my eyes, I couldn't stop them.

Chapter 18

Goodbye

We had everything ready: the few clothes we could carry in our backpacks, blankets, cans of tuna, crackers, and foods that provided quick energy, like condensed milk cooked in a pressure cooker. We also packed a Bible. If we were going to survive this journey, we needed God on our side. I needed Him to give us strength.

Victoria looked sad that morning.

I kept petting her, hoping she might cheer up, but nothing I did seemed to work.

"I'll miss you too," I told her, as if she understood.

Around nine in the morning, the doorbell rang. Leila's brothers had come early to say goodbye.

"Take good care of my sister," each of them told me before leaving.

I promised I would.

A few minutes later, Celia arrived with her husband, Carlos, and their children. On most days, Celia wore bright colors—yellows, reds, blues—but that morning she was dressed in black and looked deeply troubled.

While Victoria had hidden under the bed during the brothers' visit, when she heard Celia's voice, she came out and stood beside me.

At the door, Celia wrapped her arms around her sister.

Chapter 18

"Ay, Leila," she said, her voice trembling. "You always find a way to worry me. But this time..."

"Celia, don't be so dramatic," Leila replied, opening the door wider and letting everyone in. "I'll be fine, big sister."

I shook Carlos's hand and hugged Celia and the children. They sat on the sofa, but Celia kept talking.

"I keep hearing horror stories about that trip north," she said. "It's dangerous. Your children need you, Leila. You have to survive for them."

"Do you want some coffee?" Leila asked.

"No. I already had two cups before leaving the house. And don't change the subject."

Leila sighed.

"I just don't want to be sad. We've had enough sadness with Mami and Raúl."

"And now you're leaving the rest of your family to walk into hell," Celia replied. "You don't know who's hiding in those jungles. People die there all the time. They find bodies every day. Why do you think they call the Darién Jungle the Route of Death?"

"I have a phone, don't I?" Leila said with a faint smile.

Celia stared at her.

"You think there's phone service in those jungles?"

She shook her head slowly.

"If Mami and our brother are watching us from heaven, I ask them to protect you... And you too, Joel. You've been a blessing in our lives."

My eyes filled with tears.

"Take care of my sister," she added.

I nodded.

"I want both of you to come out of those jungles alive. Call me whenever you can."

Her children, now teenagers, were quieter than usual. The youngest, Julio, sat fidgeting with his fingers and knocking his knees together until his mother signaled him to stop.

"Are we going to see you again?" he asked, looking first at me, then at Leila.

I nodded.

"I hope you'll come visit us someday," I said.

Julio shook his head.

"Everyone leaves," he said quietly. "Grandma died. Our uncle died. My cousins moved to Argentina. This sucks. I'm running out of family."

"It doesn't matter where we are," I said. "We'll always be your family."

A heavy silence filled the room.

"What time will the driver arrive tomorrow?" Celia finally asked.

"Six in the morning," Leila replied.

"Do you have enough money?"

"Celia," Leila said gently, "we saved everything we could. We sold our cars and anything else we could sell. If it's not enough, we'll figure something out."

"Like what?"

"Plan B," Leila said.

"And Plan C," I added. "We can always find work under the table if we run out of money."

"And where will you stay?" Celia asked.

"In a park," I said. "Or wherever we can find space. We won't be the only ones making this journey."

"I know that," she replied quietly. "And I also know how many people never make it."

"Can we please talk about something positive?" Leila said. "Stop worrying so much. I'm a fighter, Celia. You know that. And I'm tired of watching Joel live like a modern-day slave."

She looked at me.

"The Cuban government has started sending reincorporated doctors back to Cuba. It's only a matter of time before they come for him. You know what that would mean."

Celia glanced at me and said nothing.

"Twelve years waiting to be free, Celia," Leila continued softly. "Twelve long years."

"I know," Celia replied. "I understand. But you can't ask me not to worry. That's what I do. I worry about everyone. I worried about Mom... about our brother... about you after your divorce..."

"You're the glue that holds this family together," Leila said.

Celia lowered her eyes.

"But I failed."

I stood up.

"Let me bring the beers a friend gave us yesterday," I said. "Kids, do you want some Toddy?"

They nodded. It was the perfect excuse to step away from a conversation that was tearing me apart.

I walked into the kitchen. Victoria followed and sat on the small rug by the sink.

"You want something to eat?" I asked her. "Are you thirsty?"

She looked at me silently, her tail still.

"I'm sorry, Victoria," I whispered. "I'm going to miss you."

Chapter 18

Guilt weighed heavily on me—not only because of Victoria.

Celia didn't deserve this.

She was one of the kindest people I had met since leaving Cuba. And meeting me had brought her nothing but pain.

I couldn't save her mother. I couldn't save her brother. And now, I was taking away the only sister she had left.

Chapter 19

The Only Option

I often asked myself, "How did I end up here?"
Could there have been another path to freedom?

In truth, there were no simple answers. The Cuban experience is shaped not by a single decision but by a chain of defining events—political, economic, and personal—that leave people with few choices.

On January 12, 2017, the United States ended the "wet foot, dry foot" policy, an interpretation of the Cuban Adjustment Act that had allowed Cubans who reached U.S. soil to remain in the country. Those intercepted at sea were returned to Cuba, but those who reached land were granted the opportunity to stay.

With that policy gone, the door that many Cubans had relied on for decades suddenly closed.

Then the pandemic arrived.

When international flights stopped in 2020, life on the island deteriorated rapidly. On April 14 of that year, DHL suspended operations in Cuba due to strict border closures imposed by the Cuban government. For many families, this meant that relatives abroad could no longer send basic goods—food, medicine, clothing—that had become essential for survival.

Conditions worsened.

Chapter 19

In January 2021, the Cuban government devalued the peso by more than 2,300 percent in response to massive budget deficits. The exchange rate shifted dramatically, from 1 CUC equaling 1 U.S. dollar to roughly 24 pesos per dollar. Overnight, prices surged beyond what most Cubans could afford.

The pandemic, combined with the repressive policies of Miguel Díaz-Canel's government, pushed the population to the brink. Medicines disappeared. Food shortages became routine. Power blackouts lasted for hours, sometimes days.

Desperation spread across the island.

People wanted to leave—by any means necessary.

When President Biden took office and migrants began arriving in large numbers at the U.S.–Mexico border, thousands of Cubans asked relatives abroad to finance flights to countries such as Panama or Nicaragua. From there, they began the long journey north, joining migrants from across Latin America who were moving toward the United States.

The larger the migration became, the more money there was to be made.

Human migration turned into big business throughout Central America.

For many Cubans, it became the only remaining path to freedom.

Yet what awaited them on that path was far worse than most could imagine.

Before long, I would learn that for some migrants, drowning at sea—or even facing sharks in the open ocean—might have been a kinder fate than

Chapter 19

the horrors that awaited in the jungles and lawless towns of Central America.

Chapter 20

Leaving Punto Fijo

José, our driver, arrived at six in the morning, just as planned. Leila and I climbed into the back seat with our backpacks and large bottles of water.

"Good morning," he said, smiling at us through the rearview mirror. "Did you sleep well?"

"We did. Thank you," Leila replied.

Before starting the car, he turned around in his seat.

"As we agreed, it will be $300 for the gentleman and $74 for the lady."

He was charging me more because I was Cuban. According to him, the extra money would ensure my safe passage to the border without problems. My upbringing in a small Cuban town and my religious faith had made me far too trusting.

I was about to learn my lesson.

Surprised that he wanted the full payment in advance, Leila and I exchanged a quick glance. We didn't want him to see where we kept the money, so I signaled discreetly to her where it was hidden.

The driver kept watching me through the rearview mirror while Leila, outside his line of sight, retrieved the cash.

When she finished counting it, she handed it to me, and I passed it forward.

"Please count it," I said.

"I trust you," he replied, still watching me through the mirror.

"I insist," I said. "In Cuba, we have a saying: clear accounts preserve friendships."

He shrugged.

"Fair enough."

He counted the money slowly.

"It's all here," he said finally, placing the car in drive.

As we left the place where I had lived for six years, I didn't feel nostalgic. I felt relieved.

Leila, however, stared silently out the window. After a while, she wiped her eyes. I patted her back and gently caressed her arm. She kept looking outside, determined to absorb every detail of the landscape—just as I had done the day I left Cuba.

We spoke very little during the drive.

Both of us were nervous about the police checkpoints we knew we would encounter.

At the first few stops, the officers didn't ask for my papers. I considered myself lucky.

That changed when we reached Río Limón.

Río Limón lies in northwestern Venezuela. The river that bears its name flows from the Motilones Mountains into the Caribbean Sea. Along its banks, indigenous communities build their homes on stilts among mangroves teeming with crabs and fish.

In 1987, devastating floods destroyed much of the region and caused significant loss of life. More than thirty years later, the scars were still visible.

It was in this town—already marked by tragedy—that the police ordered us out of the car.

They took us into a small office and began questioning us. When the officers examined my documents, one of them frowned.

"We need to call the Cuban G-2 in Caracas immediately," he said. "They will come pick you up. You cannot continue."

My stomach dropped.

"Don't do that," our driver said quickly. "Look... I can give you five dollars."

The officer stared at him coldly.

"Are you trying to insult me?"

Then he turned to another officer.

"Call the G-2 right now."

The second officer started to leave.

"Wait!" I shouted. "Please, don't call anyone."

Turning to the first officer, I said quietly, "Let's talk. You and I. We can work something out."

It was widely known that Cuban intelligence agents—the G-2—operated inside Venezuela. They had enormous influence and a reputation for destroying anyone who crossed them.

If they caught me, my life would be over.

The officer and I stepped into a small office, away from the others.

"I know where you're going," he said. "Don't think I'm stupid. You're heading to the United States."

"I don't think you're stupid," I replied calmly. "But that's not my plan. My destination is Colombia. I want to work there and send money home to our children."

He narrowed his eyes.

"I don't believe you."

Chapter 20

"I'm not saying I wouldn't continue north someday," I admitted. "But that kind of journey requires money I simply don't have."

He said nothing.

"I know things are difficult here in Venezuela," I continued carefully. "Inflation is hurting everyone. Maybe we can help each other."

I paused.

"Would $150 solve this problem?"

He shook his head slowly.

"I'm risking a lot for you. I could go to jail."

"$200," I said. "That's the most I can offer."

He studied my face for several seconds.

Finally, he sighed.

"Fine."

I handed him the money.

A few minutes later, Leila, the driver, and I were back in the car.

As I sat down beside her, I exhaled deeply.

But this was only the beginning.

***

After driving about 270 kilometers, we reached the La Guajira Desert near the Colombian border.

The way José glanced at me when the officer stopped us—and the text message he sent just before another policeman walked straight toward my door—made something painfully clear.

Our driver had sold us out.

The officers ordered Leila and me out of the car. José drove away without looking back.

Chapter 20

They led us behind a tree, out of sight of the road.

That's when the negotiations began.

At first, they demanded $2,500.

When I explained that I didn't have that kind of money, I offered $200. They refused. Their tone grew more threatening. They talked about tying me up, about beating me.

Leila pleaded with them.

"We have two children. Please let us go."

"We need the money," the older officer replied.

Then he pointed to two men.

"You two stay here with her."

He turned to me.

"You come with me. Bring your backpack."

"Please," I said, "let my wife come with us."

"She stays."

I looked at Leila. Tears filled her eyes.

"I'll be back," I said.

"Please do," she whispered.

We walked toward the road where two more officers stood beside a police car.

"You see that car?" he asked.

I nodded.

"Get in the back seat."

"Where are you taking me?"

"Stop asking questions."

Once I was inside, he left the door open and stood outside.

"Give me your phone."

I handed it to him.

"Password."

I typed it.

He began scrolling through my messages and photos, searching for anything that might reveal hidden money.

"Who are these?" he asked, pointing at pictures of Leila's children.

"Our kids," I said.

He dumped my backpack onto the seat.

"Where is the money?"

"I already gave you $200."

"I know you have more."

He leaned closer.

"Other Cubans who passed through here got tied up and beaten. Don't make me do the same."

His eyes told me he wasn't bluffing.

"I might have a little more," I said slowly. "Inside the Bible."

I handed him the $100 hidden there.

"Now we're getting somewhere," he said with a grin.

His phone buzzed. He read the message, then looked at me.

"Your wife must really love you."

"Why do you say that?"

"She just found another $300."

He chuckled.

"She bought your freedom."

I closed my eyes for a moment. This stop alone had cost us $600—money we desperately needed for the journey ahead. But the alternative would have been far worse.

The officer allowed me to repack my things and walked me back to Leila. When she saw me, she ran forward and hugged me.

Chapter 20

"Are you okay?" she asked. "Did they hurt you?"

"No, my love. I'm fine."

"I had no choice," she said through tears. "I was so scared."

"You did the right thing."

"I love you."

"I love you too."

"Isn't that sweet?" the officer said.

"Here's what will happen now. We'll drive you in the back of the police car with your hands behind your back, so the other checkpoints think you're in custody. Then we'll drop you about a kilometer from the border. An indigenous guide will take you across."

"Thank you," I said.

"You're very kind," Leila added.

I clenched my fists.

Later, I understood his real reason: if another checkpoint stopped us, we could report him. He wanted to remove that possibility.

After a short drive, he stopped and opened the door.

"You lovebirds can go now," he said. "I hope the desert and the jungle won't kill you. It was a pleasure doing business with you."

He drove away. After he left, we paced on the grass. Now what? We looked at each other, then at our surroundings. We were in the middle of no-where.

At last, we detected movement, and an indigenous man appeared from behind the trees.

"Come with me," he said.

"How much?" I asked cautiously.

"Twenty dollars."

"We might be able to manage that."

"Follow me."

We walked nearly a kilometer along dusty back roads under the scorching sun.

Finally, we entered Maicao, a border town in northern Colombia. Ahead of us stood a Colombian police officer.

"Leila, let's hide," I whispered.

Our guide stopped and turned.

"Don't worry," he said calmly. "You're safe now."

The officer took our documents and examined them carefully. Leila held her breath. He flipped through the pages again, his expression unreadable.

For a long moment, he said nothing. Then he handed them back.

"Welcome to Colombia," he said. "What brings you here?"

"We're just passing through," I replied.

He nodded.

"I hope you have a safe trip. Thank you for visiting."

I stared at him in disbelief.

"Thank you," I said. "You're very kind."

He smiled and wished us luck.

For the first time in years, we were no longer looking over our shoulders.

Chapter 21

From Medellin, Colombia, to the Jungles of Panama

Maicao was founded in 1927. During Venezuela's oil boom in the 1970s, the small border town transformed into an important commercial hub. Today, contraband flowing through the Guajira Peninsula has turned its center into a busy and chaotic marketplace. Small vendors line the streets selling fruits, vegetables, fish, and clothing from makeshift stalls.

From the center of town, we boarded a bus bound for Medellín's Terminal del Norte. The journey covered nearly 920 kilometers (572 miles) and normally took about 15 hours, but road construction slowed us down.

At one point, the police stopped our bus.

Chapter 21

My body froze. Memories of our encounters with Venezuelan police rushed through my mind. But when the Colombian officer checked our documents, he glanced at my Cuban passport and handed it back without comment.

Seventeen hours after leaving Maicao, we finally arrived in Medellín.

The terminal was modern and clean, with restaurants, showers, medical services, and dozens of people moving in every direction. For the first time since leaving Venezuela, we felt safe.

We paid a few dollars to shower, then went to a restaurant called *La Fonda del Pasajero*.

I ordered a traditional *bandeja paisa*—rice, beans, arepa, chorizo, ground beef, egg, plantains, and salad. Leila ordered grilled chicken with similar sides.

After hours of surviving on crackers and water, we devoured the food as if we had not eaten in days.

From Medellín, we boarded another bus to the coastal town of Necoclí, the last stop before the Darién Gap.

Necoclí sits on the eastern shore of the Gulf of Urabá and is home to a large Afro-Colombian population descended from enslaved Africans. Because of its proximity to Panama, it has become a major crossing point for migrants.

Sometimes the number of migrants passing through exceeds the town's capacity. People sleep wherever they can—churches, beaches, parks, or overcrowded hostels. In 2021, the town's water system even collapsed under the pressure of the massive influx.

Chapter 21

Despite its role as a gateway to one of the world's most dangerous migration routes, Necoclí is beautiful. White sandy beaches meet the turquoise waters of the Caribbean Sea.

Yet its beauty was overshadowed by the migrants' desperation, who arrived exhausted, hungry, and full of hope.

I imagined that when they fell asleep in the parks or on the beach, they dreamed of distant lands to the north—places brighter and freer than anything they had known.

***

While in Necoclí, we contacted a coyote, a guide who claimed he would take us through the jungle. He placed us in a small hotel and provided food.

The next morning, while we were eating breakfast, he asked for the full payment.

After we handed him the money, he stood up.

"I need to make a phone call," he said.

We never saw him again.

Realizing we had been cheated, we prepared to continue on our own.

We bought supplies: water, flashlights, canned beans, bread, tuna, *panela* for quick energy, snake repellent, burn ointment, rubber boots, and a tarp to sleep under.

From Necoclí, we took a small bus to Turbo, another port town on the Gulf of Urabá.

Turbo was chaotic. Vendors shouted over each other, selling tickets for departing boats. The air smelled of fish and salty seawater. The locals seemed friendly, but some men leaned against the walls near the docks, watching newcomers more than the boats.

For a fee, a guide led us to a beach where wooden boats called *cigarretas* departed for Capurganá, one of the last Colombian towns before the Panamanian border.

About twenty of us boarded a two-engine boat—Venezuelans, Cubans, and Chinese migrants.

At first, we traveled close to the coast. But the guide soon received word that the Colombian coast guard was nearby.

He steered us toward the open ocean.

Soon, the shoreline disappeared.

The waves grew violent, tossing our small boat like a toy. Some passengers became seasick. The man in front of me vomited, and the spray carried it onto my arm.

Saltwater crashed over us as the boat rose and plunged violently into the troughs of the waves.

At one point, the boat slammed down so hard it felt like hitting concrete. Then we heard a crack, and water began pouring in.

Panic spread through the passengers. The guide handed us buckets, and everyone started bailing water.

For a moment, we believed we were going to die.

Leila and I exchanged a look that said everything. Our journey might end here.

I thought of my parents. They would never know what had happened to us.

But instinct took over.

We kept bailing water.

Finally, one of the men managed to plug the hole. After exhausting minutes of fighting the incoming water, we emptied most of the boat and continued the journey.

We had survived.

The trip lasted from 2:30 p.m. until midnight.

***

We finally arrived in Chocuna, where indigenous guides waited for us.

They led us through narrow jungle paths in total darkness.

The deeper we walked, the heavier our backpacks felt. The only light came from a small flashlight carried by our guide.

Along the trail, we saw something that froze our blood.

Bodies.

Men, women, even children.

"Oh my God," Leila whispered. "They just leave them here?"

"Who would bury them?" I said quietly. "The jungle is their grave."

The Darién did not discriminate. It killed people of every age and nationality.

To survive, we had to lighten our load. We abandoned most of our clothing and kept only one change of clothes.

Leila used some of her clothes to cover the body of a young woman we passed.

When we finally reached a river around one in the morning, we washed off the salt from the ocean. Then we ate crackers with tuna and sprayed mosquito and snake repellent before sleeping under our tarp.

I felt feverish but tried to ignore it.

Sometime during the night, a jaguar approached our camp. Our guide whispered to us to stay completely still. We couldn't run. Jaguars chase prey that flees.

I held Leila's hand. Her palms were cold and damp.

Eventually, the animal left. Only then did I fall asleep.

***

We woke at 5 a.m.

Although I felt sick, we had to keep moving. The longer we stayed in the jungle, the greater the danger.

The Darién was like entering another world.

The dense canopy blocked the sunlight. Massive trees intertwined overhead, trapping us in humid darkness.

Armed groups hid in these forests, preying on migrants. Our guide told us about women who had been raped and travelers who had been murdered.

We walked in single file through deep mud that threatened to swallow our boots.

A Haitian man slipped and died when a stick pierced his neck. An Arab boy fell into a ravine.

Death was everywhere. To survive, we had to become numb to it.

The jungle smelled of wet earth, rotting wood, and humidity. During our rest stops, Leila suffered terrible headaches that sometimes made her cry. I feared they were lingering effects of COVID.

All I could do was hold her and tell her it would pass.

***

That night, my fever became worse.

I was shivering while my body burned with heat. Leila was freezing, so I lay on top of her to warm her with my body.

We survived that night by crying quietly, speaking little, and eating almost nothing.

At one point, we encountered eight Cuban doctors who had become lost and were nearly dehydrated.

"Do you have any food?" one of them asked when he heard my accent.

We shared our tuna and *raspadura* with them. In return, they gave me medicine to reduce my fever.

Throughout the journey, we continued sharing our food with others—even dividing a single can of tuna among eight people.

As a doctor and as a human being, I could not watch others die.

But helping them also meant risking our own survival.

***

It took us four days to cross the Darién Gap. Others took up to seven.

I spent the entire journey battling illness.

We spoke very little, and when I did, I used a Venezuelan accent. I didn't tell the other doctors I was Cuban until after we left the jungle.

The guide charged $50 for Venezuelans and $150 for Cubans.

I didn't want him to discover the truth.

***

The day before we exited the jungle, indigenous villagers served us a meal for five dollars.

The food tasted terrible, but we ate it politely.

"What is it?" I asked afterward.

"Turkey," the guide replied.

"Turkey?"

"A flying turkey."

Later, I realized what he meant. They had fed us vultures.

That night, everyone felt sick and gassy. But somehow, we survived.

Before leaving the jungle, the other doctors and I exchanged contact information.

If we survived the rest of the journey, perhaps one day we would meet again—somewhere far away from the jungle that had almost killed us.

Chapter 22

Panama

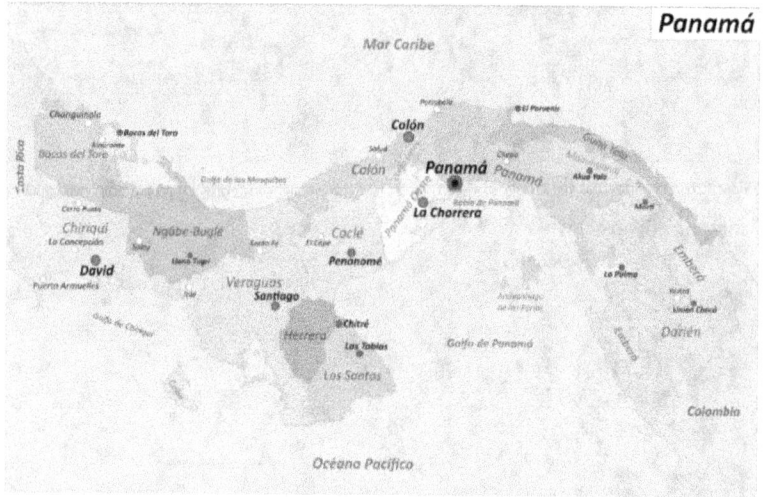

Imagenes.noticias.com

After we finally emerged from the Darién Jungle, the indigenous guides handed us over to the Panamanian military. Soldiers loaded us into the back of a military truck, and we drove for what felt like hours along rough roads until we reached a United Nations camp.

For the first time in days, we could breathe.

The camp buzzed with exhausted migrants—mud-covered clothes, hollow eyes, people sitting on the ground trying to recover from the jungle. Volunteers gave us food, and medical staff treated those who needed help. We charged our phones, grateful to see the screens light up again.

A doctor examined me and prescribed antibiotics for the cold that had been worsening during the trek. My body felt drained, but at least we were safe for the moment.

A few hours later, after authorities collected our demographic information, they directed us onto a bus heading toward the Costa Rican border. The fare was $45 per person. It felt like another tax on survival, but we had no choice.

We left in the afternoon. The bus moved slowly through the Panamanian countryside while most of us sat in silence, too tired to talk.

We arrived the following day.

There were three main crossings between Panama and Costa Rica: Paso Canoas, Río Sereno, and Sixaola–Guabito. Each had different operating hours, and Panama was one hour ahead of Costa Rica—something migrants quickly learned could mean the difference between crossing or being forced to wait another night.

Sixaola–Guabito, on the Caribbean coast, was popular with tourists. Río Sereno–San Vito lay in a mountainous region between the Caribbean and Pacific sides of the border. It was not a tourist route and not used for cargo, so it tended to be quieter.

Paso Canoas, near the Pacific coast, sat along the Inter-American Highway, part of the Pan-American Highway that stretched from Panama City to Mexico. It was the busiest of the three crossings. On the Costa Rican side stood a lively town full of duty-free shops and restaurants. On the Panamanian side, there were mostly immigration offices.

That would eventually be the crossing we used.

Our bus stopped at another camp where officials checked our documents again. The purpose was simple: to make sure no one had disappeared along the way.

When a Panamanian officer reviewed our papers, his expression suddenly hardened as he looked at my wife.

"You will be deported," he said flatly.

My wife stared at him in disbelief. "Why would you deport me?"

"This migration route is for Cubans, Haitians, and people from other countries—not Venezuelans," he said. "You have twenty-four hours to leave the country, or you will be deported."

"She's my wife," I told him.

The officer barely looked at me.

"As I said," he replied coldly, "twenty-four hours."

When we stepped away from the table, my wife's face showed the fear she was trying to hide.

"What are we going to do?" she asked quietly.

I forced myself to sound calm.

"Relax," I told her. "Nothing will happen. In a couple of hours, we'll be in Costa Rica."

Inside, however, I knew that on this journey anything could happen.

Nearby, another soldier was arguing with a Venezuelan family. Their daughter—no more than seven years old—stood beside them.

"What's happening in Venezuela is your parents' and grandparents' fault," the soldier said harshly. "They didn't dare to remove those people from power."

The girl had long black hair pulled into a ponytail and wide brown eyes. She looked at him with confusion, as if trying to understand why a grown man was blaming her family for something so far beyond her control.

Then she turned toward her parents.

Hearing the soldier's words, anger rose in me. I couldn't stay silent.

Just loud enough for him to hear, I said to my wife, "Noriega didn't stay in power because of the gringos. Panama is lucky the United States removed him in 1989."

Manuel Noriega—once an ally of the United States—had been overthrown during the American invasion of Panama and spent the rest of his life in prison. Clearly, the young soldier did not know his own history.

I had no intention of insulting Panamanians. Most of the people we met were kind and welcoming.

But no adult should speak to a child that way.

After leaving the camp, we climbed into a crowded van that took us to David, a relatively prosperous city in western Panama. From there, we boarded another bus heading to Paso Canoas.

When we arrived, the border town was chaotic.

Men approached us immediately, offering to take us to the Costa Rican side.

"Ten dollars!" one shouted.

"Twenty!"

"Sixty!"

The prices changed with every step we took.

Chapter 22

The huge differences made us suspicious. We had already been deceived too many times during this journey, and we had almost no money left.

We stood on the sidewalk in the crowded border town, discussing what to do while drivers continued to compete for our attention.

Then we noticed something curious.

A group of migrants walked into a nearby small store. A few moments later, they didn't come back out.

We looked at each other and followed them inside. That was when we realized something unexpected: the store had an exit on the other side—directly in Costa Rica.

No guards. No fees. Just a door.

We walked through.

After everything we had endured—the jungle, the fear, the exhaustion—the border turned out to be nothing more than a doorway.

And just like that, we were in Costa Rica.

Chapter 23

Costa Rica

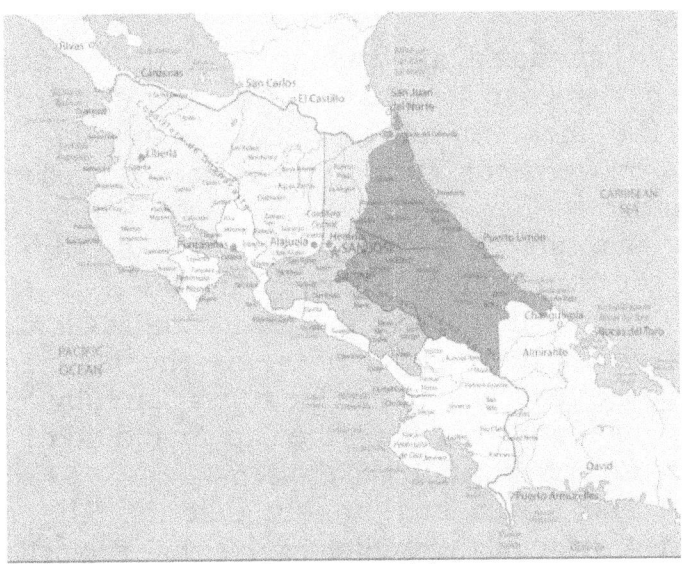

Imagenesnoticias.com

By February 2022, we had already survived the Darién Jungle, but the journey north was far from over.

Costa Rica greeted us with mild weather. During that time of year, temperatures usually ranged from about 65°F at night to around 80°F during the day. Under normal circumstances, it would have been perfect traveling weather.

But Leila could barely walk.

Her feet were badly swollen from days of hiking through mud, rivers, and steep jungle trails.

Chapter 23

Each step brought a wince of pain to her face. The skin around her ankles was stretched tight, and the flip-flops she wore barely fit anymore.

We had no choice but to stop, except that we had almost no money left.

Without money, the journey north would end here.

I contacted my cousin in the United States, and he agreed to send us $500 through Western Union. That money meant everything—it was the difference between continuing our journey or becoming stranded.

We hired a taxi to take us to Río Claro, the nearest town with a Western Union office.

The distance from the border to Río Claro was only about twenty-one miles. As the taxi moved along the road, I watched the turns carefully, mentally calculating how long the trip should take.

Something didn't make sense.

The driver kept taking detours. The road twisted through unfamiliar routes that seemed unnecessary. The ride grew longer and longer.

Then it became clear.

He was stretching the trip to charge us more.

When we finally reached Río Claro, we hurried into the Western Union office to retrieve the money.

The taxi driver waited outside, leaning against his car.

Once we stepped out with the cash, he demanded his payment—about $200.

Nearly half of what we had just received.

I felt anger rise inside me, but there was nothing we could do. We paid him.

Then he tried again.

Chapter 23

"I can get you two bus tickets to the Nicaraguan border," he said. "Thirty-five dollars each."

This time, I looked directly into his eyes.

I saw the lie before he even finished speaking. "No," I told him.

Later, I went to the bus station myself and bought the same tickets for about $15 each.

Río Claro was a small, quiet town named after the river that flowed through it before emptying into the Golfo Dulce estuary, also known as *The Point*. Tourists came there to watch surfers ride the waves or to see monkeys playing along the riverbanks.

But we were not tourists. We were migrants trying to survive the journey north.

We had only planned to stay one night so Leila could recover.

Yet when we arrived at a small hotel, the staff hesitated before giving us a room. Who could blame them? Leila and I looked like people who had been sleeping outdoors for days—our clothes caked with dirt, our flip-flops worn thin, our hair tangled and unwashed.

For a moment, the receptionist studied us with suspicion. Then she disappeared and returned with the manager.

After some pleading, the manager finally agreed to give us a room.

For $25, we got a place to sleep and transportation the next morning.

That night, the smallest comforts felt like luxuries. Hot water running down my back in the shower. Clean sheets.

A mattress soft enough to forget, for a few hours, the jungle and the road.

Chapter 23

The next morning, we ate breakfast in town before boarding a bus headed toward the Nicaraguan border.

The ride lasted almost fifteen hours.

When we stepped off the bus, several migrants stood around, uncertain about where to go. We asked the locals where to find *la trocha*, and they immediately understood.

La trocha. The dirt road.

Route 1855 stretched deep into the countryside—a 160-kilometer gravel road cutting through pineapple plantations and thick tropical vegetation. The path was difficult to locate, hidden among fields and scattered homes.

The air smelled of damp soil and fruit. Wooden houses leaned crookedly among the greenery. The reddish soil of the road contrasted sharply with the surrounding jungle.

Occasionally, trucks loaded with pineapples passed us, leaving clouds of red dust in the air.

After a few kilometers, we reached a collapsed bridge. Beyond it, the trucks turned back. From then on, only migrants continued along the path. We began walking in the afternoon, trying to keep pace with a group that seemed to know where they were going. The road climbed slowly over a mountain.

By the time the sun began to set, we reached a ranch house already crowded with migrants.

Inside, dozens of people were lying shoulder to shoulder across the floor.

We paid about $90 to sleep there and for a guide who would lead us the following morning.

As Leila and I sat quietly in a corner of the crowded room, I wondered who actually owned the place. The people collecting the money might have been squatters.

Late that night, a sudden noise shattered the silence. A sharp crack against the wooden wall.

Then another. We realized it was rocks.

Someone outside was throwing rocks at the house. The impacts echoed through the room.

Everyone froze, and a baby began to cry softly.

Were they bandits? Would they break inside?

For several minutes, the rocks continued striking the walls. Then, just as suddenly as it had begun, the noise stopped.

Slowly, the room relaxed again. Exhaustion eventually overcame fear, and people drifted back to sleep, but none of us truly felt safe. After all, we were surrounded by strangers. Someone could easily rob us while we slept.

Later, we would hear stories about thefts and assaults that had happened inside that very ranch.

But that night, nothing happened to us.

At some point during the night, I dreamed about the United States.

It was the place where my cousins—and some of Leila's relatives—had already begun new lives.

Since childhood, I had often felt that I didn't belong anywhere. The sound of those rocks striking the walls felt like a reminder of that.

The United States represented something different: Freedom.

While living in Venezuela, I once read a line from Emma Lazarus's poem *The New Colossus*:

"Give me your tired, your poor, your huddled masses yearning to breathe free."

She wrote those words to raise money for the pedestal of the Statue of Liberty.

If the United States accepted me, I hoped that one day I could stand before that statue myself.

After so many years working in the medical field, I wanted to repay that country for the opportunity to live there.

The thought of reaching that land helped me conquer my fears that night.

Before dawn, I woke up thinking about something I had read years earlier.

In 2015, nearly 2,000 Cuban migrants became stranded at the Costa Rica–Nicaragua border after Costa Rican authorities dismantled a human-smuggling network. The migrants had flown to Ecuador, one of the few countries at the time that did not require visas for Cubans.

Costa Rica eventually issued them temporary visas so they could continue their journey north. But Nicaragua refused to let them enter.

The Nicaraguan army pushed them back with rubber bullets and tear gas, creating a political crisis between the two countries.

As I remembered that story, I wondered what had happened to those migrants.

Before sunrise, still exhausted, we resumed walking.

Hours later, we left the road and followed a narrow trail toward a river.

At the riverbank, we paid a man about $20 each to take us across by boat.

The river was the Río Frío, born on the slopes of the Tenorio volcano and flowing across the plains before joining the San Juan River in Nicaragua.

Chapter 23

The boat glided quietly through the dark water.

Along the banks, we saw caimans resting on fallen logs and herons standing motionless as they hunted for fish. The river was home to more than three hundred species of animals.

The jungle around us was alive.

But our minds were focused on only one thing: the border.

Finally, the boat touched the riverbank. The motor fell silent, and for a moment the jungle seemed to hold its breath.

We stepped out of the boat and onto the muddy ground. A simple sign mounted on a concrete post marked the border.

Nicaragua.

We had crossed another invisible line on the map.

The river behind us separated two countries, but it also separated two chapters of our journey.

Ahead of us stretched another unknown road—another country, another set of dangers, another group of people who might help us or exploit us.

By then, we had learned some important lessons:

Every border carried its own risks. Every mile demanded another sacrifice.

Still, we kept moving forward.

Because turning back was no longer possible.

The road to the United States was still thousands of miles away, and Nicaragua would test us in ways we could not yet imagine.

But one thing had already become clear to us.

Chapter 23

Freedom was never given.

It had to be earned—step by step, mile by mile, border by border.

And Nicaragua was waiting.

Chapter 24

From Nicaragua to Honduras

Map from Wikipedia

The boat left us on the banks of the San Juan River in Nicaragua. The motor faded into the distance, leaving us surrounded by the jungle's sounds.

From there, we began walking through mangroves and dense forest in the direction the captain had indicated. Before leaving us, he had pointed down a narrow trail and said that after about a kilometer, we would find a house where we could buy food.

We adjusted our backpacks and started walking.

Chapter 24

The air was heavy with humidity, and the ground was soft beneath our feet. Mosquitoes buzzed around us as we moved deeper into the vegetation.

After a while, I turned to Leila.

"How are you feeling?"

I already knew the answer, but I wanted her to know that I cared about her well-being.

"Tired," she said quietly. "I miss the kids and my family."

"I'm sorry," I replied. "I had no other choice."

"You keep telling me that," she said. "I know. If we make it, it will all be worth it. I just hope I don't disappoint you."

"You could never disappoint me."

For a moment, we walked in silence, our footsteps mingling with the rustling leaves around us.

Then we heard voices. We froze.

Ahead of us, partially hidden behind shrubs and trees, several soldiers appeared. They were wearing fatigues and carrying AK-47 rifles slung across their chests.

My heart began pounding in my ears.

Without speaking, we crouched behind a thick cluster of bushes. I gently pulled Leila closer to the ground, trying to make us as invisible as possible.

The soldiers moved slowly along the path, talking among themselves. Their boots crunched in the dirt just a few meters away. One glance in our direction and they would see us.

We barely dared to breathe.

After what felt like an eternity, the voices grew fainter, and the soldiers disappeared down the trail.

Chapter 24

We stayed hidden for several more minutes, just to be sure. Only then did we stand up and continue walking toward the house.

When we arrived, a husband and wife were waiting there. They greeted us warmly and, for a few dollars, sold us some vigorón—crispy fried pork served with yucca—along with bottled water.

After hours of walking, the food tasted incredible.

For the first time that day, we felt a small sense of relief.

Before we left, the husband pointed us toward another group of men who could help migrants bypass the nearby immigration checkpoint.

The men wore military-style uniforms, though it was impossible to tell whether they were real soldiers or simply smugglers posing as such.

For more than $100 each, they offered to take us on motorcycles close to the checkpoint and explain how to get around it.

We had little choice but to trust them.

The motorcycles sped down narrow dirt roads, the wind hitting our faces as we held tightly onto our backpacks.

Before reaching the checkpoint, the drivers stopped.

From there, we continued on foot, quietly circling through brush and trees until we were safely past it.

Once we cleared the checkpoint, we boarded a bus.

Later, we got off near Palo Negro and began walking again—this time through the night to avoid the next checkpoint.

Chapter 24

Eventually, we reached Managua, the capital of Nicaragua, located on the southern shore of Lake Managua. Founded in 1819, Managua is the largest city in the country, home to more than a million people. Much of it had been rebuilt after a devastating earthquake, and fire destroyed large sections of the city in 1931.

By the time we arrived, we were exhausted, hungry, and nearly penniless.

Fortunately, before leaving Costa Rica, we had arranged for family in Miami to send us more money through Western Union. After collecting the money, we finally ate a proper meal and found a cheap motel to rest for the night.

The next morning, we boarded another bus heading toward the Honduran border.

Friends traveling on a bus ahead of ours stayed in contact with us, warning us about police checkpoints along the road.

Around two in the morning, before reaching the next checkpoint, we got off the bus.

For the next four hours, we walked through the forest to avoid the police. The darkness was overwhelming.

Every sound seemed louder at night. Branches snapped beneath our feet. Insects buzzed around our ears. Somewhere in the distance, an animal cried out.

My imagination began to race. What if a jaguar appeared? What if a venomous snake were hidden along the trail? Out there, anything could happen.

Still, as we thought about our families, we kept walking. We had to make it—for them and for ourselves.

Chapter 24

Around six in the morning, we finally emerged from the forest and returned to the road. There, we boarded another bus whose driver was coordinating with the driver from the first bus.

The second bus dropped us off near a narrow dirt trail.

To reach Honduras, we would have to walk nearly twenty-four hours along that isolated path, doing everything possible to avoid contact with the Nicaraguan authorities.

When we finally crossed the border into Honduras, several men on motorcycles appeared almost immediately.

They offered to take us to the nearest village.

Another border behind us. Another uncertain road ahead.

But by then, we had learned something important. Every step north brought us closer to the life we dreamed of. And farther away from the lives we had been forced to leave behind.

Chapter 25

Honduras

Border towns in Honduras were overwhelmed with migrants crossing from Nicaragua, many hoping to continue their journey to the United States. In recent months, however, large numbers of Nicaraguans had also begun crossing through hidden trails to avoid immigration procedures and receive the COVID-19 vaccine in Honduras.

Many migrants who intended to continue north eventually ran out of money and became stranded in Honduras. With nowhere else to go, they depended on charitable organizations that were increasingly overwhelmed and had fewer resources to respond to the growing migration crisis.

Chapter 25

But Honduras was not a safe place to remain.

As of 2021, the country had a homicide rate of 56 per 100,000 people—the second highest in the world. Theft accounted for nearly half of all reported crimes. It was clear to us that we needed to remain alert and move on as quickly as possible.

Fortunately, we had family and friends in the United States who were willing to lend us money. We promised them that once we found work in the United States, we would repay every dollar.

Still, we had already asked for far more help than we had expected.

Our first stop in Honduras was the city of Choluteca, located in the southern part of the country near the borders with Nicaragua and El Salvador. The city served as a major access point to the Pan-American Highway. The Choluteca Bridge, with its distinctive silver arches, spanned the river leading into the city.

Although it was the seventh largest city in Honduras, it had fewer than 100,000 inhabitants. The region lay in the lowlands surrounded by mountain ranges—typical of Honduras, where nearly two-thirds of the country is mountainous.

After arriving in Choluteca, we did something that felt almost surreal after weeks of hardship: we ate burgers and fries at a Burger King.

Then we rented an inexpensive room for the night.

As I lay in bed staring at the ceiling, Leila stepped into the bathroom to take a quick shower. We had traveled so far and survived so much, yet the journey was far from over. Anything could still happen before we reached our destination.

Chapter 25

The past few weeks had been among the most difficult of my life.

Quietly, I prayed for the strength to face whatever challenges still lay ahead.

The next morning, we left before sunrise in a van that cost about $90 per person. Prices varied widely for migrants, especially Cubans and Venezuelans. Drivers competed for business, some asking $50, others $150 or even $200.

It was difficult to know whom to trust.

The van carried us along a clandestine mountain road toward the Honduran terminal. As we drove through the mountains, we saw something disturbing through the window.

Groups of criminals were attacking migrants who had no choice but to cross the mountains on foot.

Some were robbed. Others were beaten. Many had their belongings taken from them.

Watching those scenes reminded us how fortunate we were to have found transportation.

From the terminal, we purchased bus tickets to continue through the towns and villages of Honduras.

At our first checkpoint, we were treated surprisingly well. A man who looked and sounded American appeared to be supervising the officers there.

"Where do you come from, and where are you going?" he asked.

We told him the truth.

He nodded and allowed us to continue without any problems.

The next checkpoint was very different.

Chapter 25

After examining our passports, the officer openly demanded money. Eventually, he forced each of us to pay $100 before allowing the bus to move forward.

From that point on, things only got worse.

Every couple of kilometers, there seemed to be another checkpoint. Even when the police did not initially stop us, the driver would communicate with them using hand signals.

The officer would then wave us down.

The bus door would open.

And the police would climb aboard to collect money from the migrants.

At one of those stops, a woman sitting a few seats away from us pleaded with an officer.

"Please, sir," she said. "We are traveling with children, and we haven't eaten. Have mercy on us."

I will never forget the man's response.

"I don't care," he said coldly. "My heart is black and made of stone. The only thing that speaks to me is money. Either you pay me, or you won't continue."

The woman began to cry.

With trembling hands, she opened her wallet and gave him the little money she had left.

And the bus moved forward again.

Chapter 26

Guatemala

In January 2021, a caravan of thousands of Honduran migrants heading north toward Mexico and the United States confronted soldiers and police in riot gear in the town of Chiquimula, in southern Guatemala. Authorities used tear gas and struck migrants with batons to stop them, but the migrants eventually broke through the police lines.

Now, more than a year later, the constant flow of migrants had not slowed.

I often wished I had been born in a democratic country instead of a place consumed by the poison of totalitarianism disguised as communism. I missed the land where I was born. I missed my family.

But I needed to be free—even if it cost me my life.

In Guatemala, it almost did.

I must have eaten something that had not been cooked properly because I suddenly became very ill with fever and severe diarrhea. We had no choice but to rent a cheap room where I could recover.

Leila didn't know what to do.

She looked desperate as she watched me bent over the toilet, soaked in sweat. Soon, the chills set in, and my body began shaking uncontrollably.

I knew that if I didn't stay hydrated, I could die.

The problem was that I couldn't risk going to a hospital to receive intravenous fluids. That would expose us to immigration authorities.

I asked Leila to go to a nearby pharmacy to buy oral rehydration fluids and any other recommendations from the pharmacist.

For two days, I felt as if death were knocking at my door.

At last, on the third day, I was able to keep down a little food, though I tried to stick to a bland diet. Once I regained some strength, we resumed our journey toward Mexico.

But not before becoming victims of unscrupulous men willing to do anything for money.

My weakened condition clouded my judgment when I agreed to pay a man $300 after he promised to take us safely to the Mexican border and guaranteed that no one would stop us.

While we were on the bus, that same man sent a message to someone through WhatsApp.

By mistake, the message appeared on my phone before he deleted it.

In the message, he gave the authorities my name and physical description and asked them to stop our bus because I had money.

When I confronted him, he shrugged.

"Well," he said casually, "there are bad people here. That's true. But in Mexico, it will be worse."

It took everything I had to remain calm. I couldn't afford to lose control. I had to focus on the bigger goal.

I needed to get out of Guatemala.

Chapter 26

Long-term planning was no longer possible. Survival meant focusing only on the next small victory.

That day we ate almost nothing.

A Cuban man sitting across the aisle overheard Leila whisper that she was hungry.

"I feel so weak," she said.

I had nothing to give her.

"I'm sorry, my love," I told her quietly. "We ran out of food."

She began to cry, and I felt completely helpless.

"Where are you from?" the man asked from across the aisle. "You sound Cuban."

I was relieved that we were seated near the back of the bus. I nodded and placed my index finger across my lips, asking him silently not to speak too loudly.

He understood immediately and smiled.

"I'll share some bread with mayonnaise that I brought with me," he said.

"Are you sure?" Leila asked.

"We have to help each other," he replied.

After my illness, I was afraid to eat anything with mayonnaise, but the burning pain in my empty stomach was becoming unbearable.

It was a choice between risking getting sick again or continuing to starve.

I took a small bite.

Several hours later, we arrived in San Marcos, a city in southwestern Guatemala along the Sierra Madre de Chiapas.

After leaving the bus, we hired a rickshaw-style tricycle taxi that carried us about fifty kilometers toward the banks of the Suchiate River near the town of Tecún Umán.

This crossing point handled the largest flow of migrants traveling from Guatemala into Mexico.

The town itself was named after Tecún Umán, one of the last rulers of the K'iche' Maya people, who was killed by the Spanish conquistador Pedro de Alvarado in 1524.

When we reached the riverbank, several indigenous men were waiting with rafts.

They ferried migrants across the Suchiate River, which marks the southwestern border between Guatemala's department of San Marcos and Mexico's state of Chiapas.

We climbed onto one of the rafts and drifted slowly across the muddy water.

When we stepped off onto the opposite shore, we both exhaled deeply.

At last, we had arrived in Mexico.

Chapter 27

Tapachula, Mexico

Source: Bing.com -free images - iStock

After crossing into Mexico, Leila and I joined a group of migrants who took a van from the border city of Hidalgo to Tapachula.

As the van moved along the road, I stared out the window. The paved highway stretched ahead of us, lined with green shrubs and trees. Small houses appeared here and there, and people walked along the roadside going about their daily lives.

I tried to focus on the scenery to calm my thoughts.

Inside, however, I was panicking.

I had read reports that the Mexican National Guard had become increasingly violent as illegal immigration surged. During confrontations with migrants, guards had beaten men so badly that some lost several teeth.

I tried not to imagine the worst.

What if Leila were hurt?

What if we were arrested?

On the way to Tapachula, we passed several checkpoints where police demanded money to let us continue. By the time we arrived in the city, we had no money left.

Without money, we could not pay for transportation, food, or the bribes that seemed unavoidable along the route.

But there was another obstacle: We could not continue our journey without first obtaining a temporary visa.

Getting one, however, would prove far more difficult than I expected.

Tapachula was a busy city with paved roads and rows of one- and two-story buildings. Located along the Coatán River, at about 449 feet above sea level, it sits on the Pacific coastal plain and serves as the region's main commercial and manufacturing hub.

Yet despite its size, the city felt overwhelmed.

We were still thousands of miles from the United States. The driving distance between Tapachula and the Mexicali border was more than 2,500 miles. For a Mexican citizen, the trip might take three or four days.

For migrants like us, it could take weeks—or even months.

Tapachula had around 360,000 residents, but with the constant arrival of migrants, the population had grown dramatically. Shelters built to house 400 people were now holding five times that number.

Many migrants slept in parks, shelters, or directly on the streets, risking arrest by police or the National Guard.

We felt trapped.

Outside the city, multiple checkpoints prevented migrants from traveling north without proper documents. The only way out was to obtain a visa—or somehow find enough money to continue the journey through illegal routes.

But the generosity of family and friends had limits, and we had already reached them.

If we tried to leave without documents and were caught, we could be sent to the immigration detention center known as Siglo 21.

The stories about that place terrified me.

The facility was notorious for overcrowding, poor food, and a foul smell that filled the building due to poor hygiene. Migrants held there were often denied access to lawyers. Attorneys who tried to visit were sometimes told their clients did not want to see them.

Guards would pretend to call the detainees and then return to the attorney, saying, "I kept calling him, but he didn't answer."

A lie.

Corrupt officials reportedly demanded between $1,500 and $2,000 to release detainees.

For them, lawyers were bad for business.

Some friends who had been detained there were eventually deported back to Cuba because they could not pay.

The thought made me tremble.

Chapter 27

Not Cuba.

I would rather die than go back.

When Leila and I arrived at the INM immigration office, we saw a seemingly endless line. More than a thousand people were already waiting.

We joined the line.

Soon, the couple standing in front of us introduced themselves. They were Venezuelans who had experienced many of the same hardships we had faced along the journey.

That conversation marked the beginning of a friendship.

Behind us stood a Haitian couple. They spoke little Spanish but knew some English. Sometimes they answered us in Creole, and we managed to understand each other through gestures and smiles.

The woman, Fabiola, had kind eyes and spoke more than her husband. Later, I would come to believe that God himself had sent this beautiful Haitian woman in her forties.

The line lasted for days.

We slept on the sidewalk at night and stood in line from six in the morning until midnight.

By the second day, we had no food left.

Reluctantly, I asked my cousin to send us a small amount of money for food and for the visa application. Leila held our place in line while I went to the bank to collect the money.

When the woman at the counter saw my Cuban passport, she shook her head.

"I cannot process transactions for Cuban nationals," she said.

I didn't understand.

Why would the bank refuse Cubans?

Confused and discouraged, I returned to the line.

When Fabiola heard what had happened, she immediately offered to help.

She left her husband holding their place in line and accompanied me to the bank. My cousin then sent the money to her name instead of mine.

This time, the bank handed her the cash without hesitation. I was stunned. When we left the bank, I tried to give her some of the money, but she gently refused.

"No, thank you," she said.

She placed one hand on her chest and then softly pressed the other against mine.

I understood her gesture.

"It's a gift," she meant.

After everything we had endured, it felt as if God had placed an angel in our path. Fabiola radiated kindness and generosity.

Rumors circulated constantly among the migrants waiting in line. Some said that even a visa did not guarantee safe passage. There were stories of Cubans who had been deported despite having valid documents.

The uncertainty filled me with anxiety.

During the five days we waited in line—eating little and standing under a relentless sun—my body began to show signs of stress.

One afternoon, I ran my fingers through my hair and froze as large clumps came loose between my fingers.

"Leila, look," I said.

"It's your nerves, my love," she replied gently.

Around us, the suffering continued. Children cried from hunger.

One woman collapsed from exhaustion, and I rushed to help her. Fortunately, I still had oral rehydration packets in my backpack, so I gave them to her.

Sleeping on the hard concrete sidewalk tested my ability to adapt, but I found comfort in knowing that we were surrounded by people who understood our struggle.

On the fifth day, when we finally received our visas, we embraced our new friends and exchanged phone numbers.

It was time to go our separate ways.

We wished each other luck and promised that, if fate allowed, we would meet again one day—this time in the United States.

After saying goodbye, Leila and I wandered through the crowded streets until we found a cheap motel.

I asked to speak with the manager.

A man in his late fifties came out and listened as we explained our situation.

After a moment of thought, he offered us a simple arrangement: we could clean rooms in exchange for a place to sleep and a little money.

It was more than we expected.

For five days, we had slept on sidewalks without showers. Our bodies carried the sour smell of sweat and dust.

The chance to bathe and sleep in a bed felt like a blessing.

The room was small. A single bed with a curved mattress stood against the wall, covered by thin sheets and worn pillows. A faded blue curtain hung over the window, smelling faintly of mold. A small gas stove sat in the corner, but it was broken.

The next day, I asked the manager if I could borrow some tools to try to fix it.

When I succeeded, he asked if I could help with other repairs.

Soon, I was fixing plumbing, ceiling fans, electrical problems, and broken furniture—skills I had learned while living in Venezuela.

For the first time in weeks, we had a roof over our heads and a small way to earn money.

And for the first time since arriving in Tapachula, hope returned.

Chapter 28

The Dream

In my dream, we had been living in the United States for ten years. I was working again as a doctor and owned a cozy house in southwestern Miami. Leila's children were married and had already given us grandchildren. We all lived close to one another, and Leila and I watched our growing family with pride.

My parents still lived in Cuba, in the same town and house where they had spent their entire lives. I had often asked them to come live with us in the United States, but they always refused. They said they were too old to begin again in a new country. By then, they were already in their seventies.

On the first day of our summer vacation, Leila and I traveled to Cuba to visit them.

When Mami opened the door, I was startled by how thin and wrinkled she looked.

"Mami!" I said. "It's me—Joel."

"Joel!" she cried, opening her arms wide.

She embraced me tightly and covered my face with kisses while Leila stood nearby watching us, tears running down her cheeks.

My own tears blurred my vision.

"Mami," I whispered, "I have dreamed of this day for so long."

"For more than twenty-two years, my son," she said softly. "More than twenty years waiting to see you walk through this door again."

She cupped my face in her hands and looked at me with loving eyes. Her hands were rough from years of working in the fields with my father, and she smelled faintly of onions.

"But what are we doing standing here?" she suddenly said. "Come inside! Let me call your father."

She turned toward the back of the house.

"Lorenzo! Where are you?" she shouted. "Come out here. Joel is here. Our son has come home!"

A moment later, I heard the familiar sound of my father's wooden sandals scraping across the floor. He had made them himself years ago. Even though I had sent him a brand-new pair of shoes, Mami said he still preferred his old wooden ones.

Finally, he appeared in the doorway.

I had waited so long for that moment—to embrace him again. I stepped forward. But just before I reached him, I heard Leila's voice.

"Joel," she said gently. "It's time to wake up. We have to get ready for work."

I opened my eyes.

The faded blue curtain of the motel room came into focus.

For a moment, I stayed still, trying to hold on to the dream. But reality slowly returned.

We were still in Tapachula.

Chapter 29

The Border

Several weeks passed, and our savings remained meager. Leila's family eventually realized that at this pace, we would never be able to leave Mexico. Even though they could barely afford it, they agreed to send us money—money they had to take from their own food and necessities. This time, Leila went to retrieve it.

By then, we had been in Tapachula for five weeks, hiding from authorities and limiting our trips outside the motel. We often saw other migrants detained by the National Guard or beaten in the streets. Having a visa did not always guarantee safety. Fortunately, when we had to run errands, we could leave our belongings in the room, allowing us to walk around the city looking like ordinary residents.

By the sixth week, we still had no idea how we would ever leave Tapachula. The money we received from family wasn't enough.

Then something unexpected happened.

A woman in Tampa, Florida—a friend of my cousin—sent me $2,500. She told me I could repay her whenever I was able.

When I received the money, it felt as if the heavens had opened.

At last, we could leave.

It was April 2022.

Chapter 29

We tried taking a taxi to the bus station. Normally, the ride costs about $2.50. As soon as we got into the back seat, however, the driver must have noticed my Cuban accent.

"It's fifty dollars," he said.

"How can it be fifty?" I protested. "It's supposed to be two dollars and fifty cents!"

"Either you pay me fifty," he replied calmly, "or I report you to Immigration."

At that moment, something inside me snapped.

"Leila, let's go," I said.

We grabbed our bags and stepped out of the taxi. I walked around to the driver's window and shouted in my unmistakable Cuban accent.

"You want to call Immigration? Go ahead! Do it!"

Leila stared at me in disbelief. I wasn't sure whether she was shocked by the driver's threat or by the fact that she had just seen me lose my composure for the first time.

The driver cursed and sped away.

A minute later, I waved down another taxi. This time we were charged the correct price.

From the bus station, we boarded a bus bound for Mexico City, about 721 miles away—a trip that would take roughly seventeen hours. By the time we paid for the bus tickets and passed through multiple checkpoints where corrupt officers demanded money, more than a third of the $2,500 was already gone.

Mexico City overwhelmed me.

The vast metropolis pulsed with color and life. Murals decorated the walls of old buildings, churches rose above crowded streets, and the central plaza buzzed with activity.

Yet as we walked toward our next bus connection, I felt small and insignificant in the middle of such an enormous city. But we were only passing through.

Our next destination was Mexicali—the final stop before the border.

I was nervous.

After everything we had endured, I feared that something—or someone—would disrupt our plans at the last moment. My profession as a doctor had taught me patience, but this journey had repeatedly tested it.

And I was nearing my breaking point.

The journey to Mexicali covered about 1,640 miles and would take nearly thirty hours. It was a long trip along roads filled with checkpoints.

Our Venezuelan friends were traveling on a bus ahead of ours. They stayed in contact with us by text message. They had left several hours earlier and were already approaching Mexicali when police stopped their bus.

During the inspection, officers discovered drugs on board, and my friends feared they would all be arrested.

Police searched everyone on the bus. Later, I would learn just how invasive those searches were. After nearly an hour, the bus was allowed to continue.

As our own bus moved north, I could feel the acid building in my stomach.

The checkpoint before Mexicali shocked me.

Chapter 29

Police ordered every passenger to undergo a cavity search.

They even removed the diaper from a crying baby girl to inspect her.

During that stop, officers confiscated the remaining $2,500 that the woman in Tampa had sent us.

I had never experienced such humiliation.

One officer stood in the aisle in front of me, while another blocked the row behind me. A third conducted the searches.

When it was my turn, they ordered me to unzip my pants. I had to stand there while a stranger touched me in ways no human being should have to endure.

It was degrading. But what angered me even more was when they began searching my wife.

"I want a female officer," I demanded.

"There isn't one," the policeman replied.

I clenched my fists as the man searched her. My breathing grew heavy, thick with rage. Leila noticed. She placed her hand gently over mine and shook her head.

Don't.

The frustration inside me rose like lava in a volcano. I had never felt so powerless.

Three days after leaving Tapachula, we finally arrived in Mexicali. During that time, we had barely eaten and had not bathed once.

With no money left, we went to the San Juan Refuge.

An employee there asked if we could contribute a donation to help cover the cost of gas for the stoves and the tortillas they prepared for the growing number of migrants.

"I'm sorry," I said. "I have no money right now. But I will pay you next week. I will call a friend."

I could no longer ask my family for help. My conscience wouldn't allow it.

A friend in the United States agreed to send Leila $500. After picking it up from Western Union, we paid the woman at the shelter.

But the remaining money was not enough to hire a coyote to guide us to the border.

We would have to find our own way.

For the next few nights, we slept on the floor in a large, windowless room crowded with men, women, and children. The few bunk beds available were reserved for women.

At least we had bathrooms and could eat each day.

Still, the crowded conditions meant we risked catching COVID-19 at any moment.

While at the shelter, we met a Honduran migrant named Sergio. A drug cartel had abducted his family.

"Don't pay a coyote," he told us. "I know how to reach the border."

I didn't trust him. I didn't trust anyone anymore.

Sometimes I listened quietly to his phone calls, trying to determine whether he was telling the truth. When Sergio stepped away one day, Leila whispered to me:

"What if he trades us to the cartel to get his family back?"

Chapter 29

She had a point. I knew nothing about this man. Still, when Sergio finally left the shelter, we made our decision. We followed him.

It was a leap of faith.

We boarded a bus bound for *Los Algodones*, the town closest to the border in the Mexicali region. Ninety minutes later, we arrived.

As we walked through the small town, Sergio said quietly:

"We must reach the river. The wall there is incomplete."

We left the paved streets and crossed empty land near the border. The sandy soil was strewn with abandoned documents, clothes, and shoes—left behind by migrants who had come before us.

Soon, other migrants joined us. Then more.

Suddenly Sergio turned.

"Hurry," he said. "Too many people will attract the police. This will be their last chance to take our money."

We began walking faster. Behind us, I saw mothers carrying children, men traveling alone, couples holding hands.

Then we heard shouting.

"Stop!"

Several Mexican police officers were running toward the migrants behind us.

"Run!" Sergio yelled.

Leila and I ran toward the river.

Across it, on higher ground, I could see the border wall. One section was missing—a break in the barrier.

Sergio pointed.

"You see that opening?"

Chapter 29

"Yes!"

"That's freedom. Hurry!"

We ran.

Ahead of us was a shallow river filled with rocks.

"Careful, Leila!" I shouted, grabbing her hand as we crossed through the current.

Once on the other side, we ran again.

Two officers stood near the opening in the wall.

We sprinted toward them, gasping for air.

"You can stop running!" one officer shouted in Spanish.

"No! Police are chasing us!" I said frantically.

"Sir," he said calmly, "you made it. They cannot touch you now. You are safe."

"We... we did?" I asked.

"Yes.

Welcome to the United States of America."

For a moment, I stood frozen while tears filled my eyes. I dropped to my knees and kissed the ground.

I was in the United States. My childhood dream had finally come true.

I was free.

Leila knelt beside me, hugging me as she cried.

"We made it, my love," she whispered. "We made it."

I stood and embraced her while Sergio watched quietly. I turned toward him and gave him a grateful nod.

Then I thought of my parents.

Chapter 29

My phone battery was nearly dead as I dialed a neighbor's number.

Julio answered on the second ring.

"Julio, it's Joel. I'm calling from the United States. Please let me speak with my parents."

"The United States?" he exclaimed. "You made it to the Yuma! Your parents are here. They arrived a few minutes ago."

He passed the phone to my mother.

"Joel?" she said softly. "Is that you?"

"Sí, Mamá."

"I haven't heard from you for weeks. I was so afraid something had happened to you. I prayed every day. Are you okay?"

"Sí, Mamá. We made it. We're in the United States."

"You didn't tell me what you were doing," she said. "I was so scared."

"I didn't want to worry you," I replied, glancing at my dying phone battery. "Vieja, please put Papá on. My battery is about to die."

A moment later, my father's voice came through.

"Son... you made it?"

"Sí, Viejo. My dream came true."

"I knew it," he said proudly. "I told your mother not to worry. You're my son. I knew you would never give up."

I stood there in silence for a moment, holding the dark phone in my hand.

The call had ended, but my father's words remained in my mind.

You can do it.

For years, he had shouted those same words to me from the riverbank while teaching me how to swim as a boy in Cuba.

At the time, I thought he was only talking about the water. Now I understood he had been preparing me for something much bigger.

I looked around me.

The sun was beginning to set over the desert landscape. The air felt different on this side of the border. Not because the land had changed—but because my life had.

For the first time in decades, I was standing on free soil.

The road that brought us here had taken us across jungles, rivers, mountains, and deserts. We had crossed countries where strangers showed us kindness and others tried to take advantage of our desperation. We had endured hunger, fear, humiliation, and uncertainty.

Many times, along the way, I wondered whether we would survive the journey. Many others had tried this same path and never made it.

I thought of the migrants still walking somewhere along that long road north—men and women chasing the same dream that had brought me here.

Freedom.

I turned to Leila.

She was still holding my hand, as if afraid that if she let go, the moment might disappear like a dream.

"We made it," I said softly.

She smiled through her tears.

"Yes," she whispered. "We did."

Behind us lay thousands of miles of hardship.

Chapter 29

Ahead of us lay a new life we would have to build from the beginning.

But for the first time in many years, I felt something I had almost forgotten.

Hope.

And as I stood there on the soil of the United States, I finally understood something my father had been trying to teach me all along.

Sometimes the river looks too wide. Sometimes the current is too strong. But if you keep swimming, you will reach the other side.

Epilogue

Two months after Joel's arrival in the United States, seventeen Cuban physicians attempting to escape their medical missions in Venezuela were arrested. Some were deported back to Cuba, where they are expected to face prison sentences of up to eight years for abandoning their assignments.

One physician still stationed in Venezuela spoke anonymously about the conditions they endure:

"We live in misery. This is hell. They have taken our passports, and Cuban and Venezuelan military guards watch the borders to prevent us from leaving. We are treated like slaves. Our labor generates income for the Cuban government—that is why they detain us."

For decades, the Cuban government has sent thousands of doctors and medical professionals abroad as part of its international medical missions. While the program is often presented as humanitarian aid, many physicians who have participated describe a different reality—one in which the government keeps most of their salaries and severely restricts their freedom of movement.

Dr. Camacho, the physician whose story inspired this novel, plans to petition for political asylum for himself and his wife once he has saved enough money to cover the legal costs.

Epilogue

Like many Cuban doctors who have fled these missions, he hopes to rebuild his life in freedom and continue practicing medicine without fear.

He and many of his colleagues continue to appeal to the international community to examine the conditions under which these missions operate and to ensure that no physician anywhere in the world is forced to work under conditions resembling modern slavery.

Joel's journey may have ended when he set foot on American soil, but the struggle faced by many Cuban doctors continues.

Even today, thousands remain trapped in foreign countries, working under strict government control, separated from their families, and afraid to speak out.

Their stories are rarely told.

But they are still waiting—for freedom, for justice, and for the day when no doctor will have to risk everything to live with dignity.

Joel made it to freedom.

But thousands of others are still walking the road.

Acknowledgements

I want to express my deepest gratitude to the individuals and organizations whose support made this book possible.

My special thanks go to **Yasek Camacho Alonso** for sharing the powerful and important story on which this novel is based, and to his wonderful wife, **Sary Pachay**, for contributing her testimony to one of the chapters.

I am grateful to **Dr. Allen Witt**, retired president of Hillsborough Community College and lead author of *America's Community College: The First Century*, for writing the heartfelt introduction to this book.

My sincere appreciation also goes to **Susana Mueller of Susanabooks** for designing the beautiful book cover and for serving as a thoughtful beta reader of this manuscript.

I would also like to thank **Conchita Hicks**, another beta reader, who provided valuable comments and suggestions that strengthened the manuscript.

My thanks extend to the **Facebook group All Things Cuban** and to its administrator, **Alex (Alexander Diaz)**, for providing an important forum dedicated to sharing Cuban history and culture.

To my husband, **Ivan**, thank you for your thoughtful suggestions on various chapters of this book. Your insights and encouragement were invaluable. I am also grateful to my **mother-in-law, Madeline; my son, Ivan, and his wife, Gloria; and**

159

my brother, Rene, and sister, Lissette, for their support and contributions.

I would also like to thank the members of the **Women Reading Great Books** group for their continued encouragement and support.

Finally, I extend my heartfelt appreciation to **all the readers who continue to support my work**, share my posts, and to the many **book clubs that have selected my books**—far too many to mention individually.

This book also benefited from research and information found in the following articles and sources:

Cuba's Biggest Exports Are Doctors Adjudged One of the Best in the World. Here's Why – Face2Face Africa

How Education Shaped Communist Cuba – The Atlantic

Cuban, Russian, and Chinese Military Presence in Venezuela's Armed Forces – Diálogo Américas / Voz de América

Periodista dice que campamento de migrantes de la ONU en Panamá se está ampliando – April 18, 2022

Costa Rica's Border Road, "La Trocha," Confounds – Tico Times (2015)

Cuban Migrants Paralyze Nicaragua–Costa Rica Border – Blanca Morel, Marco Sibaja, Ezequiel Becerra (November 18, 2015)

How Bad Is Crime in Honduras? – November 28, 2021

Additional sources consulted:
Cubanet.org
AmericaTeVe.com

Acknowledgements

To everyone who helped, supported, and believed in this project—thank you.

Other Works by the Author

Betty's stories have reached readers around the world, from the award-winning *Waiting on Zapote Street* to the No. 1 new releases *The Girl from White Creek* and *The Pedro Pan Girls: Seeking Closure*.

Her other works include:

Brothers: A Pedro Pan Story

Havana: A Son's Journey Home

The Dance of the Rose

Under the Palm Trees: Surviving Labor Camps in Cuba

Candela's Secrets and Other Havana Stories

Love Letters from Cuba

A Girl Named Polina

These books are available in both English and Spanish.

Waiting on Zapote Street received the Latino Books Into Movies Award and has been selected by numerous book clubs, including a United Nations women's book club.

Betty's work has appeared in several publications, including the prestigious literary journal *The Mailer Review*.

Through her writing, Betty strives to ensure that the stories of the Cuban people are not forgotten and to give a voice to those who might otherwise go unheard.

www.ingramcontent.com/pod-product-compliance
Lightning Source LLC
Chambersburg PA
CBHW071520170626
46811CB00007B/2907